Defenders of the Damned by Alan Hynd

New York: A. S. Barnes and Company, Inc.

London: Thomas Yoseloff Ltd.

Note: *In certain instances, names and locations have been changed for legal reasons.*

For NOEL of whom I am so proud

PREFACE

Sitting in my study very early of a morning or quite late of a night, when things are dead quiet and the phone is unlikely to ring, and when my wife and my daughter and my son are all safely in their rooms asleep, sheltered from the violence that stalks the land, I often fall to thinking about some of the malefactors who are, in an indirect way, the source of my livelihood. I have, for more than a quarter of a century now, been writing about the doers of evil and their dark accomplishments for such magazines as the *American Mercury*, *Coronet*, *Cosmopolitan*, *Esquire*, *Reader's Digest*, *Saturday Evening Post*, and *True*. In fact, it weren't for the satanic practitioners of murder, mayhem, and mystery, I could very well be writing about, Heaven forbid, the history of corporations or the feeding habits of beetles.

If, then, I am indebted, however obliquely, to the criminals, I am, by similar reasoning, beholden to their lawyers. For if it weren't for certain types of lawyers—criminal lawyers in every sense of the word—many a malefactor would think twice before going out and fracturing a statute. What, though, with a cunning, highly-paid mouthpiece, adept at oratory, pulling the yarn over the eyes of morons on the jury while an ungifted political hack, playing the role of an assistant district attorney, stands helplessly by, the criminal frequently has the best of it and murder won't out.

Who, then, were the greatest criminal lawyers? The three greatest, in the first half of the twentieth century in this land of ours, were, in my opinion, William J. Fallon, Clarence Darrow, and Earl Rogers. Curiously enough, and perhaps fortunately enough, Fallon, Darrow, and Rogers operated in different sections of the country—Fallon in the East, Darrow in the Middle West, and Rogers on the Pacific Coast. I tremble to contemplate what would have happened to The Blind Goddess had Fallon, Darrow, and Rogers functioned simultaneously in one section of the country.

They were different kinds of men, these three, in vital respects. Fallon, the New Yorker, seldom studied a case thoroughly, if at all, before going into court with it, depending on his charm and his brains and his theatrics for an acquittal. Rogers, in Los Angeles, was, on the other hand, the meticulous researcher and seldom stepped into a courtroom without knowing considerably more about the issue at bar than anybody else present. Darrow, in Chicago, was something of a cross between Fallon and Rogers. Darrow was, to my mind, also a split personality—half the courtroom magician pulling rabbits out of the hat for the jury, and half the completely dedicated crusader for the forgotten and faceless little man.

I am indebted to *True—The Man's Magazine,* in which these three works first appeared, for permission to put them together in this book.

Alan Hynd

Westport, Connecticut
July, 1960

CONTENTS

Contents

Defenders of the Damned

EARL ROGERS

Earl Rogers, the great Pacific Coast mouthpiece, had just sat down in his office in Los Angeles one morning in 1915 when a sharply dressed stranger entered.

"Mr. Rogers," asked the man, "is it true that you've gotten more'n a hundred acquittals in murder cases?"

Rogers, measuring the stranger as he dragged on a cigarette, nodded.

"Good," said the man, reaching into his pocket for a fat roll of gold-backs. "How much will you charge to defend a man for killing somebody who's been running around with his wife?"

"My retainer fee is usually $5,000," answered Rogers. "The balance depends on the nature of the case."

The stranger peeled off five grand, handed it to Rogers, and headed for the door.

"Wait a minute," said Rogers, "Where are you going in such a hurry?"

"To kill the sonofabitch."

Rogers jumped up and grabbed the man. "Hold on," he said. "I am not *that* good."

Earl Rogers just could have been wrong, for once. In a

quarter century of handling murder cases he ran up a total of 183 acquittals against less than a score of convictions.

Clarence Darrow, one of the cagiest attorneys ever to pull the wool over the eyes of a jury, called Earl Rogers the greatest lawyer he has ever seen in a courtroom. When, in fact, Darrow himself was indicted on a charge of buttoning up a deal with a juror, he screamed for Rogers to defend him. And Rogers beat the rap.

Like William J. Fallon, the great mouthpiece of New York (the only man in the same league with him), Earl Rogers was a great hand for liquor and the ladies. But unlike Fallon, Rogers was painfully careful in preparing a case. Fallon depended almost solely on remarkably fast thinking and the spell his Irish charm cast on jurors. Rogers added to a lightning mind and devastating personal charm an infinite capacity for research and a unique talent for locating loopholes in the laws.

Some prosecutors thought Earl Rogers always purchased at least one juror in his toughest cases. Once, when twelve men brought in a murder acquittal for Rogers, an assistant prosecutor cracked, "The bastard has bought all twelve this time." Actually, Earl Rogers never needed anything more than his courtroom oratory, skill, and trickery to accomplish his ends.

"Even when he's drunk," Bill Fallon once said, "Earl Rogers is better than any other stone-sober lawyer in the whole damned country."

Early in his career, when the crime of adultery was taken more seriously than it is today, Rogers proved that thoughtful application to the statutes was better than a purchased juror any time. He was defending an amorous gentleman and a seductive young lady who were charged by the man's frau with sharing a house in open adultery. Rogers sat calmly staring off into space as the prosecutor called to the stand the butcher, the baker, the plumber, the iceman and the cop on the beat around the love nest. Everyone claimed to have known the defendants as man and wife, an ordinary couple like most others.

When each prosecution witness had testified, Rogers intoned, "No questions, thank you."

It wasn't until the state's case was in that Rogers sprang the trap. Rising, clearing his throat, and flecking an imaginary speck from the lapel of his tailored suit, Rogers bowed to the judge.

"Your Honor," he said, "I respectfully request a dismissal of the charge against my clients."

"On what grounds, counselor?"

"On the grounds that the prosecution has proven them innocent."

The judge looked puzzled and the prosecutor dismayed. Rogers picked up a law book and began to read: "If two persons, either being married to another, live together in a state of open and notorious adultery, each is guilty of a felony." He closed the book and calmly looked up at the judge again.

"If the court please," he declared, "my clients did not live in open and notorious adultery. They *concealed* their adultery, Your Honor, by representing themselves as husband and wife. Thus they have not violated the law."

Rogers stood there for about eight seconds longer, allowing the import of his words to register fully on the judge. Then, characteristically when he scored a point, he raised his eyebrows and shrugged.

His Honor, taken aback, retired to his chambers to consult the law. In a little while he returned.

"Case dismissed," he said bluntly.

Earl Rogers was the pioneer in compiling files on prospective jurors. He knew all about a man's politics, religion, business, and sex life before he ever asked a question. Consequently, when examining a jury candidate, he was able either to smile at the man and accept him at face value, thus flattering the fellow, or query him gently about a phase of the case that he really intended to ignore. In this way he threw the prosecution off the scent.

Before he died in 1922 at the age of fifty-two, a broken-down ruin in a flop house, Rogers ran through several fortunes. How much he made and squandered will never be known. His fees, many of which were in cash that he quickly dissipated in hitting the high spots and picking also-rans at Santa Anita, must have climbed well into the millions.

Earl Rogers was the first big-time lawyer to bring showmanship into the legal realm. He was a superb actor. Tall, thin, and pallid, he had jet-black hair, heavy eyebrows, Irish-blue eyes, and a jutting chin. He was built like a wedge, with broad shoulders, deep chest, narrow waist, and flat hips—a tailor's delight. His voice, which was to bowl over countless men—and women—was deep, rich, and perfectly controlled. When he got going in the courtroom, his words took wings.

Rogers never used profanity. The cuss word to him was the tool of the mentally disinherited. He had more than a hundred suits, and was constantly being dunned for payment by the best tailors in town. He smoked cigarettes rolled in brown paper— three to four packs a day—and frequently interrupted his own cross-examinations to run out and take a few drags. He was married twice, but never happily so for long.

A vain man, Rogers affected wine-red dressing gowns. He selected his own steaks and mixed his own salads in restaurants. He used perfume and a lorgnette. His eyesight was 20-20 and he needed that lorgnette like he needed a dent in the skull. But he employed it to stunning effect.

When, in the midst of an unfriendly cross-examination, Earl wanted to create the impression that the witness was lying, he'd whip out his lorgnette and peer at the witness in a puzzled manner. Then he'd put the glass back in his pocket and look at the jury, as though he could not understand how such statements were made and expected to be believed. Rogers often reserved the lorgnette treatment for a hostile witness who was telling the truth and apparently wanted to stick close to it.

At other times, after he had taken a man apart, he would demolish the pieces with the lorgnette. Being so close that he was practically sitting in the lap of the witness, he'd screw up his handsome features in contempt and study the man through the glass as if he were a laboratory worker eying a bug.

The trial that got Earl Rogers off and soaring was a murder case that few lawyers in Los Angeles would have handled. It grew out of a dispute between a prominent attorney, Jay E. Hunter, and a mechanic named Billy Alford over a bill Alford claimed he was owed for work. Alford, a spiteful type, opened up a regular campaign to collect. He began by parading around town wearing a sandwich board reading: JAY E. HUNTER IS A DEAD BEAT.

Since Hunter was a proud and dignified man, the mechanic figured the publicity would shame him into settling up. It did no such thing.

Next, Alford took to loitering outside the building where Hunter worked and yelling reflections on the legitimacy of the man's ancestry. Hunter, playing both deaf and blind, simply ignored him. That burned the mechanic up.

One morning Alford waited in the dark corridor outside Hunter's office and when the lawyer came out fired a single shot into him. The bullet entered Hunter's navel, took a downward course through his intestines, and went out his posterior.

When a crowd collected, there was Hunter on the floor, a real dead beat, and Alford standing over him holding a smoking heater.

Alford confessed to the cops. Then, brooding in jail, he decided his confession had been a mistake and sent out feelers for a mouthpiece. Rogers, in his twenties at the time and still scratching for office rent, rushed to Alford's cell.

After listening to the prisoner's account of the shooting, Rogers said, "I'll take the case. The first thing you're going to do is retract your confession."

"How?"

"Why," said Rogers, "that confession was *beaten* out of you."

Preparing for the trial, Rogers worked day and night reading fifty medical books, principally those showing a man's insides. He consulted with several physicians. He went to a hospital and studied a human stomach in a glass jar. When the trial began, he was loaded for bear.

By the time the state's simple but devastating case was in—built on Billy Alford's enmity toward Hunter and the testimony of witnesses who had seen the mechanic standing over Hunter, gun in hand, immediately after the shooting—Rogers was the only man in the courtroom who would have bet a nickel beer on his client's chances. When he got up to begin his defense, he began peering around the prosecution's table, looking for something.

"What is counsel hunting for?" the judge asked.

"The stomach," replied Rogers.

"The *what?*"

"The stomach of Jay E. Hunter."

Hunter's stomach was not in court, as Rogers knew. The prosecutor demanded to know why Rogers wanted it.

"Why," answered Rogers, feigning surprise, "to prove that the state's case is false. My client, Your Honor, was not *standing* when he shot Hunter. He was *lying face up on the floor.* Hunter knocked him down with the heavy cane he always carried and was leaning over beating him when my client shot in self-defense."

When Hunter was dug up and his stomach brought into the courtroom in a glass jar, Rogers took a pointer and proceeded to give the jury a lesson in anatomy.

"Now then, gentlemen," he said, "you can see by looking at Mr. Hunter's stomach that the bullet did, as the prosecution maintains, enter Mr. Hunter's navel and take a downward course.

"But notice this, gentlemen. Notice *this.*" Rogers took the jar and tipped it forward about 45 degrees. "This was the position of Hunter's stomach when he bent over to attack my client with his cane. Notice that when he leaned down, the relative positions of his insides underwent a great change to the man on the floor. When Hunter leaned over this poor man to attack him, his navel was actually lower than his posterior. Thus, when my client, lying on his back, fired upward in self-defense, the bullet entered Hunter's navel and had to travel *upward*, not downward, through his stomach, to go out his posterior."

Earl paused and waited while the lesson sank in.

"In other words, gentlemen," he went on, "a bullet fired by a man *lying on the floor* into the stomach of a man *leaning* over him will take exactly the same route through the body as it would if the man firing it were *standing on his feet* and pointing the weapon slightly downward at a person *standing* opposite him."

The jurors were so fascinated by Rogers' explanation of how the killing *could* have taken place that they never stopped to consider how it *had* taken place. So Billy Alford was acquitted of murder, and Earl Rogers, having won the case that most other lawyers wouldn't touch, was on his way.

Earl Rogers was born near Buffalo, New York, in 1870, the only boy in a family of three children. His father, the Reverend Lowell Rogers, was a Baptist minister and his mother was a part-time preacher. The parents, of English and Irish blood, wanted Earl to become a man of the cloth. A more forlorn hope could hardly ever have beat in a human breast.

Earl spent two years at Syracuse University, where he soaked up knowledge like a sponge. He could read and speak Greek like an Athenian, and he had a taste for music. But it was his quick mind and phenomenal memory that made him outstanding. Earl could glance briefly at a page, then repeat it practically word for word.

The Rogers memory was to be a vital asset to him in his career. During a big trial he often had a stenographer take down a transcript of the testimony, and during the evening he'd run through it, then hand it to his daughter Adela (who was to become renowned as the writer, Adela Rogers St. John).

"Dad paced up and down the room," Adela once said, "reeling off that courtroom testimony, while I checked what he was saying. He never forgot a single important point."

Young Rogers' parents had moved to the Pacific Coast by the time he had gone through his second year at college. They couldn't afford to send him on, so, in Los Angeles, he caught on as a free-lance reporter for several papers.

It was as a reporter that Earl Rogers developed a social consciousness. He saw life in the raw, and what he saw disturbed the Irish sentimentality in him. Impressed by the fact that many poor people died before their time because of lack of proper medical attention, he decided to become a doctor and help the

forgotten. He hoped to lay aside enough money from his newspaper work to study medicine.

And he might have—except for the usual complicating factor
—love. In California he had been regularly corresponding with
a girl back in New York State—brunette Hazel Belle Green.
One night, feeling especially lonely, he sat down and dashed off
a proposal. Hazel Belle quickly accepted and came to the coast
to marry him.

Earl's first child—there were eventually to be four—was
born within the year, and his medical hopes went glimmering.

Working as a newspaperman, Rogers got to know several
lawyers. He was bellying up to a bar with one of them one night
when the mouthpiece said, "You know, Earl, you'd make a
pretty good lawyer yourself."

Rogers thought over the remark afterward. He had already
grown tired of the newspaper life. A man with expensive tastes
and a long thirst, he couldn't see much of a future pounding a
typewriter. The law—that was something else again. He pictured himself strutting before a jury, the attention of an entire
courtroom focused on him, and he could almost feel the crisp-
ness of his fancy fees.

But Rogers had a deeper reason for embracing the law. As a
reporter, he had seen many poor wretches getting the book
thrown at them because they had bum lawyers, and watched
ambitious prosecutors build phony cases against helpless defendants.

His mind made up, Rogers started by serving an apprentice-
ship in the offices of ex-United States Senator Stephen M.
White. White was considered the most brilliant jewel in California's legal diadem—an old boy with a golden voice and a
silver tongue. From him Rogers learned the importance of
thorough preparation. When a case was not strong, White said,

the trick was to get a weak-minded jury. Rogers later improved on that approach by making a weak case *look* strong, thus, for all practical purposes, turning moronic jurors into imbeciles and imbecilic ones into idiots.

Admitted to the California bar in 1897, when he was twenty-seven, Earl teamed up with an older lawyer named Telfair Creighton. Creighton was a stiff, icy southern aristocrat who breathed such rarefied air that he never appeared in a police court. He latched on to young Rogers because White had given him a good build-up and because he needed a fellow to handle the crummy stuff that came into the office.

Earl began to represent police-court customers—drunks, call girls, pimps, and petty thieves, all snagged in the daily dragnet. The pay was narrow but the experience was wide.

One morning Earl was in court looking for clients when a busty blonde gave him the eye.

"Would you like to defend me?" she asked.

"Sure," said Rogers. "What's the charge?"

"Oh, I winked at a fellow on Fifth Street last night and he turned out to be a cop. I'm new in town."

Rogers pulled out all the stops in defending her. What right had this hateful cop to lure an innocent stranger into a trap? By the time Earl was through, the spectators thought the cop rather than the blonde was on trial. She was released, and Rogers celebrated, as he was more often doing, with a bottle.

One morning Earl checked into Creighton's office with bloodshot eyes and a breath that would wither a geranium. The older lawyer's nose shot into the air.

"I'm sick of your coming in here looking and smelling like that," Creighton said stiffly.

"And I'm sick of you," Rogers snapped.

Next day Earl was in another office—tiny, but his own.

Around the turn of the century, before Hollywood was to give Los Angeles its title as sex capital of the country, the city was already doing nicely in the carnal league. It boasted every conceivable type of joint for amatory pursuit, from cribs to parlor houses.

Earl soon became a familiar figure in them. Since news like that gets around, he explained to his wife that his presence in the red-light district was purely for professional purposes. Why he bothered to explain even he probably couldn't have said. From the first day he had appeared in a courtroom as a lawyer, he had begun to pay less and less attention to his home life.

"I never should have married," he once said to a friend. "I'm just not cut out to be a husband and father. I'm an old lone wolf."

As a matter of fact, Earl was really picking up a lot of business and getting a lot of tips—not to say making contacts—in the red-light district. The houses served a cross-section of the male population of the city as well as visiting firemen. Earl made friends with pimps and policemen, with merchant princes and lawyers, and occasionally with a judge.

One night in a parlor house an acquaintance took him aside. "Doc Crandall wants you to take his case," he said simply.

Rogers knew the story. Crandall, a physician who spent a great deal of his time trying out the antiseptics in bars, had gone off on a party nearly a year ago with a pal and a couple of girls. Doc had got in a fight with the other guy over the other's girl —one Ruby Gaines—and whipped out a rod and plugged him.

At his trial some months before, Ruby, the only witness to the shooting, had testified against him, and Crandall had been convicted. But his lawyer had got him a new trial on a technicality. In gratitude, Crandall quarreled with the lawyer, so now he got his friend to ask Rogers to represent him.

Addressing himself to the problem of a defense, Rogers came up with a simple solution. The state's whole case rested on the testimony of Ruby Gaines. Now if Ruby should fail to testify . . .

Rogers learned that she had never been in Mexico and had a passion to go there. So he made a proposition to a carefree leecher he knew.

"The night before the trial begins," he said, "I want you to take Ruby Gaines to Mexico and stay there with her until I send for you. I'll pay all expenses."

When the trial opened, Rogers, sitting beside Doc Crandall, whispered, "Say something to me. Anything at all. I want to look as if I'm worried."

Crandall obligingly whispered back and Rogers scribbled meaningless words on a pad, then ran his hand through his hair and shook his head. The prosecutor, studying the two, figured they were plenty worried. But when court opened, it was the prosecutor who sweated blood. His star witness didn't show.

The prosecutor asked a delay. Rogers objected. Objection sustained. The state's case blew up.

When it came Rogers' turn to address the jurors, he simply stood before them, raised his eyebrows and shrugged, then sat down. The jury acquitted Crandall in three minutes flat.

Although the stunt Earl had pulled was hardly a gem of originality, it did him a lot of good. It established him as a cagey mouthpiece who wouldn't hesitate to pull a fast one.

As time went on, Earl came to the attention of an old codger named Thomas Gooding. Old Judge Gooding, a dressy character who was long on righteousness and dignity, before coming to the coast, had been chief justice of the Arizona Territorial Supreme Court. After settling in Los Angeles he opened a law office and took just enough work to keep his hand in.

Gooding dropped a letter to Rogers suggesting that they meet for a drink. When they got together a day or so later they took an instant liking to each other.

"My boy," said Gooding, who was twice Rogers' age, "I think we would do quite well if we went into partnership."

Rogers was flattered. Judge Gooding, he knew, was a whizz at the fine points of law and he could absorb a lot of knowledge from the old boy. So the two shook hands on the bargain and set up shop.

It wasn't long afterward that a couple of stick-up men decided Los Angeles was just the place to carry on business. Wearing masks and flashing guns, they started operations. Their technique never varied. Functioning only at night, they hid behind shrubbery in a better residential street and stuck up anybody who hove into sight.

"A dangerous pair, that," remarked Judge Gooding, who despised stick-up men.

"They must be paying the cops," said Rogers.

The remark was entirely in order. In those days the Los Angeles Police Department was honeycombed with crooks getting rake-offs for everything from petty larceny to murder.

One night, though, when the two bandits were cleaning out the pockets of a distinguished citizen, an honest cop happened along and ran them in. The prisoners—Minter and Dodge—promptly yelled for Rogers, and he came.

"We want to get out on bail," Minter said.

"I take it you're guilty."

"Well, yes."

"Can you pay a retainer fee?"

They could pay a thousand.

The deal was on. There were just a couple of bugs in it. Rogers had to convince his righteous old partner, who wanted no truck with stick-up men, that Minter and Dodge were innocent.

Giving the judge his share of the fee, Earl told Gooding that their new clients had been framed by a glory-seeking cop.

"You're sure of that, Earl?"

"Oh, absolutely, Judge. Absolutely."

During the period Minter and Dodge were in jail, the stick-ups ceased. The judge wondered about that. Earl explained that the real culprits had been scared off by the arrests.

Rogers saw to it that his clients were arraigned before a jurist he had frequently seen in a parlor house.

"Your Honor," said Rogers, to make sure everything was understood, "I believe we have met someplace before."

The judge coughed, turned red, and said he couldn't place the face. Then he released Minter and Dodge on peanut bail.

The two immediately opened up for business again. One morning, Rogers, reading his morning paper at breakfast, almost choked on his eggs. There on the front page was an account of the latest caper of his clients. Their victim had been, of all people in Los Angeles, Earl's partner, Judge Gooding.

Shortly thereafter, the judge and Rogers went their separate ways.

Earl Rogers now began to attend all important criminal trials. Sitting as a spectator, he made notes about jurors, witnesses, judges, prosecutors, and defense lawyers. He decided that jurors were usually fascinated by medical testimony, and that defense lawyers frequently failed to take advantage of the flaws in such testimony as presented by the state.

Deciding to bone up on medicine, Rogers cultivated a couple of doctors. They described their operations and advised him on the best medical books for a layman. He haunted the accident wards of the big hospitals, not as an ambulance chaser but as a student of injuries. In time he came to know nearly as much as many doctors about the workings of the human body.

Rogers' knowledge of anatomy came in handy when he was engaged to free Jack Parsons, a lifer in San Quentin who had been sentenced for killing a man by a blow on the head. Rogers studied the record.

Parsons, when a freight conductor on the Santa Fé, had been chosen to represent his fellow workers in a pay dispute with the railroad. The railroad won and the workers accused Parsons of selling out.

One day, in the freight yards near San Bernardino, California, Parsons got into an argument with a worker named Dodd. He invited Dodd into the caboose of his train to talk things out. There was a fight in the caboose, and when it was over Dodd was lying on the floor, dead.

Parsons, at his trial for murder, had been accused of having struck Dodd savagely on the head with a heavy instrument. Denying this, the conductor claimed Dodd had been killed by accident when, during a scuffle, the man had tripped and fallen, striking his head on a pot-bellied stove.

The prosecution's big gun, Rogers saw, had been the coroner's surgeon. The doctor had sawed off the top of the dead man's head and found a piece of shattered bone within on the left side of the skull. The lethal blow, however, had been inflicted on the right side. Yet a terrific blow on the right side, the physician had maintained, could have loosened the bone fragment.

"Would an *accidental* fall have been forceful enough to produce that fragment on the opposite side?" the prosecutor had asked.

"Absolutely not," said the doctor.

And that was what had sent Jack Parsons to prison.

Rogers went to court and asked for permission to have Dodd dug up.

"On what grounds?" asked the judge.

"On the grounds, Your Honor," said Rogers, who didn't know what he would find, "that the skull of the dead man will prove my client innocent of murder."

"Request granted," said the judge.

Dodd's head had been buried with the rest of the corpse. Now Rogers had it removed. He called on a doctor and asked him to go over the skull. When the sawbones did, Rogers went back to San Quentin to see Parsons.

"You're practically a free man," he told his client.

"What will I have to do in court this time?" Parsons asked.

"Practically nothing," said Rogers. "I'm going to make the top of Dodd's skull talk for you."

Rogers obtained a new trial and his physician testified that the fragment of bone which had come loose had been detached not by a blow but by carelessness on the part of the autopsy surgeon.

"Would you mind pointing out to these fine men, Doctor" —Rogers waved a manicured hand toward the jurors—"just how the autopsy surgeon was, shall we say, careless when he sawed the top of the skull off?"

"I'd be glad to," said the doctor carefully coached by Rogers, "if I could see the top of the skull."

Rogers smiled. "Glad to oblige," he said.

He went to a small wooden box that had been at his elbow since the beginning of the trial. He reached in and pulled out Dodd's skull. Then he walked over to the jury box and held the object up before the jurors.

"A hideous thing to look at, isn't it?" he said. "But not so hideous as the sight of an innocent man spending the best years of his life behind the bars of San Quentin."

Now Rogers held the skull before the doctor. The physician pointed out just how the autopsy surgeon could have dislodged the piece of bone. The jury was soundly impressed. But Earl wasn't through yet. He put on another medical expert.

"Tell me, Doctor," he said, "would you say that the thickness of this skull is normal?"

"No," answered the witness, "it is not."

"Just what do you mean, Doctor?"

"This is a very thin skull."

"Really? Thinner than the average skull?"

"Oh, by far."

"Then a man with a skull as thin as this could easily have injured himself fatally by falling and hitting a sharp point on a stove?"

"Certainly."

Rogers looked at the jurors and shrugged his shoulders faintly. "That will be all, Doctor," he said.

Parsons was acquitted.

Earl Rogers possessed an unerring instinct for figuring out how the human animal would behave under any circumstances. This ability was dramatically revealed when he was defending a southern youth by the name of Billy Cole for the murder of a gambler known up and down the Pacific Coast as the Louisville Sport. Cole and a pal of his, a gangling weasel named Prene, had been engaged with the Sport in an all-night poker session in a hotel room on Catalina Island. The game was still going strong at dawn when somebody fired a gun twice.

The police found the Louisville Sport lying dead and Cole blaming Prene for the shooting. Prene, on the other hand, was giving Cole full credit for the job, and he was a more convincing talker. So, despite the fact that Prene's fingerprints were found on the murder gun, Cole was stuck with a murder rap.

Rogers, brought into the case for Cole, studied Prene, the state's star witness, as he unfolded his story of the shooting. Prene said that after Cole shot the Louisville Sport he pointed the gun at him. But then after holding the weapon on him for a minute or so, he shook his head and threw the revolver on the floor. Prene said he thereupon picked up the gun, and that was how his prints were found on it.

When it came his turn to cross-examine, Rogers whipped his lorgnette out and eyed Prene carefully before speaking. Turning to the jury, so that neither the judge nor the prosecutor could see his face, he screwed up his handsome features in an expression of disgust. Then sarcastically he began.

"You say that after Cole shot the Louisville Sport he pointed the gun at you?"

"That's right."

"But after pointing the gun at you for a minute or so, he tossed it to the floor and you picked it up, and that's how your fingerprints were found on the weapon? Is that correct?"

"That's right, Mr. Rogers."

"Now," Earl went on, looking at the jury, "why did Cole throw the gun to the floor instead of shooting you, too?"

"He said the Louisville Sport had cheated him. I hadn't."

"Now let me get this clear. Before he decided he had nothing against you and tossed the gun to the floor he stood there pointing the gun at you?"

"Yes, sir."

"And what did you do?"

"Nothing. I just stood there."

"You didn't scream or duck or try to do anything to protect yourself?"

"No."

"Why?"

"I guess I just wasn't afraid."

"But you were scared enough to pick up that gun when Cole decided to throw it to the floor."

"That was different."

"How?"

The witness shrugged. "I don't know. It was just different."

"But you insist that when Cole had shot and killed a man before your very eyes and then stood there pointing the smoking gun at you, you didn't do anything?"

"I didn't do a thing."

"That's all," said Rogers.

During the balance of the trial, Rogers was not quite himself. He seemed to lose interest in the proceedings. Once in a while he threw his head back and laughed, apparently at nothing. Rumors started that he might be cracking mentally.

When it came time for Rogers to sum up, he still wasn't himself. There was no sparkle in his eyes, no fire in his voice, no spring in his steps. His words weren't taking wings. The jurors stirred restlessly, obviously anxious to bring in a guilty verdict and go home.

Roger seemed to grow wearier as he rambled on and on, often wandering so far from the issue that the prosecutor asked the judge to steer defense counsel back on the track.

Suddenly, as Rogers was nearing the end of his summation, a strange, wild light came into his eyes. He began to dart glances around the courtroom, first at opposing counsel, then at the spectators, finally at the judge.

In a flash he leaped into action. He dashed over to the table where the murder gun lay, and picked up the weapon. Reaching into his jacket pocket, he brought out six bullets.

Everybody—judge, prosecution lawyer, court attendants, and spectators—stared at him, so shocked that not one moved or spoke.

Rogers quickly loaded the gun, and the strange light in his eyes grew more alarming. He let out a yell and began to jump up and down, brandishing the gun. Suddenly stopping, he started instead to breathe heavily. By now the spectators were screaming and rushing for the exits.

Rogers slowly brought the gun up to shoulder level and took careful aim at the open-mouthed prosecutor, sitting in a chair not ten feet away. The prosecutor leaped aside and fell behind a table.

Taking several quick steps forward, Rogers pointed the gun at His Honor. The judge ducked behind his bench.

Then Rogers, his eyes even wilder, ran toward the jury box. As he thrust the gun at the jurors, they yelled and tried to crawl beneath their chairs.

"Mr. Rogers!" the judge shouted, peering over the top of his bench. "*Mr. Rogers!* Put that gun away!"

Rogers turned and looked toward the court. He relaxed, dropping his hands to his sides, and a wan smile came to his face.

"With pleasure, Your Honor," he said quietly. "With the *greatest* of pleasure."

He emptied the gun, dropped the bullets in his pocket, walked over to the exhibit table and replaced the weapon. A bailiff quickly grabbed it.

Order restored, the judge demanded to know the reason for this performance.

"The *reason*, Your Honor?" Rogers asked. "Why, simply to show that the principal witness for the prosecution was lying when he said he didn't react in any way to having a man who had just committed a murder point the weapon at him.

"I beg Your Honor's pardon for having to take such extreme measures. But a human life is at stake here, Your Honor, and I believe extreme measures were justified. I wanted Your Honor and the prosecutor and the gentlemen of the jury to prove *to themselves* how a man acts under such a condition. And I believe I have established an important fact—that the state's principal witness is a perjurer—even though I had to pretend that I was not in my right mind to do it."

Acquittal, naturally.

As time went on, Earl Rogers became the confidant of practically every madam in Los Angeles and many of the girls. One of these girls was a small brunette with a strangely innocent-looking oval face. Her name was Maimie Brown and she had worked in a house in Billings, Montana, where she had come to the attention of a talent scout for the business named Happy Carlin. Happy, a greasy-haired, perfumed character had brought Maimie to Los Angeles and made a fine living pimping for her.

Chatting with Maimie one night, Rogers asked her what she wanted most out of life.

"A wedding ring."

Earl raised his eyebrows. "Yep," Maimie went on. "Me and Happy's goin' to get married one of these days and open a lunchroom. Then I won't have to do this for a livin' no more."

"You're saving your money?"

"I give everything I make to Happy," she said. "He's puttin' it in the bank for both of us."

A few nights later, Rogers got a phone call from the cops.

"We just pinched a whore, Earl," growled the desk sergeant. "She says she wants you to defend her."

"What's her name?"

"Maimie Brown."

"What's she done?"

"She just shot a man to death."

"Who?"

"Happy Carlin."

Walking into Maimie's cell, Earl asked her how it had happened. The answer was brief.

"I found out Happy was spendin' our money on another woman," Maimie explained. "So I shot him."

"How many times?"

"Once. Through the belly."

"Where'd you get the gun?"

"I went out and bought it."

"How were you carrying it? In a purse, in your pocket, or where?"

"In my muff." She handed the muff to him.

"Where'd you learn to shoot, Maimie?" Rogers went on.

"Back home in Billings."

"So when you saw Happy you pulled the gun out of your muff, took aim, and fired just once?"

"That's right."

"Who saw you take the gun out?"

"Two men."

"They've both told the police that?"

"Yup."

"They're suffering from delusions. They didn't see that gun. They only *thought* they did."

Rogers presented Maimie Brown to the jurors dressed as a Puritan maiden—black bonnet fringed with white lace, and a high-necked black dress with lace ruffles around the collar.

Tripping to the stand to testify in her own defense, Maimie looked as pure as the driven snow before it drifted. Fully prepared by Rogers, she had a terrible tale to tell—how Happy

Carlin had lured her from Montana under a promise of marriage, then forced her into a life of shame. Rogers, as he questioned his client, seemed to be fighting back tears at her story. But if he was successful in stanching a salt flow, a couple of old pots he had planted among the spectators weren't. They began to bawl out loud.

Maimie Brown went to the point where the shooting had taken place.

"And so you bought this little gun," Rogers prompted her, "to protect yourself from the beatings that the deceased was constantly subjecting you to?"

"Yes."

"And you had the little gun in your muff the day he accosted you?"

"Yes."

"And when he rushed at you with a menacing expression and foul, threatening words, you were terrified?"

"Yes."

"And then what happened?"

"Everything got blurred, Mr. Rogers."

"Did you hear your revolver going off?"

"No, sir, I didn't."

"You made no attempt whatever to take the revolver—this little weapon that you were carrying for self-protection—you made no attempt to draw it out of your muff and fire it?"

The prosecutor was on his feet, howling an objection, before Maimie had a chance to answer. Rogers appeared to be startled.

"Your Honor," cried the prosecutor, "counsel for the defendant is not sticking to the facts. He is implying that this defendant did not remove that gun from her muff when in truth she did."

Rogers went over to the prosecutor and stared at him.

"How, sir," he demanded, "can you stand there and *say* such a thing? Why, this gun went off because of my client's reflexes before she had a chance, let alone any intention, of removing it from her muff."

Now Rogers opened a small handbag and pulled out the muff. After having the defendant identify it as the one in question, Earl stepped before the jury and held it up.

"Notice," he said, "the bullet hole in this muff." Sure enough, there was a bullet hole. "And notice," he continued, turning the muff inside out, "notice the powder burn on the inside—the burn made when this poor, innocent girl, who had been led into a life of shame, fired the gun from a natural reflex induced by sheer terror of this brute who was attacking her."

And there went the state case, right out the window.

By the time he had been practicing for eight years, Rogers, now thirty-five, was a pretty heavy drinker. He was a hero in many places around Los Angeles, but not in his own home. His wife Hazel Belle, a long-suffering soul, having abandoned all hope that he would ever be much of a husband, centered her whole life about their children. But she was still open to his periodic appeals.

During a trial, Earl managed to control the bottle, but as soon as it was over, with an acquittal in the bag, he'd collect the balance of his fee and light out on a binge. Often enough he'd start out with something like five thousand dollars in cash in his pocket. A week or two later Hazel Belle would get a phone call.

"It's me, honey," he'd say. "Will you please forgive me if I come home?"

For a long time she always did.

One thing she didn't have to worry about was his secretaries.

Earl now had a office in the California Building, one of the best in downtown Los Angeles, and he worked alone there with his secretary of the moment. But he saw to it that his secretaries, who never stayed long, were ladies of spectacular homeliness. When he was studying a case, Earl didn't want any distractions. He didn't consider the bottle, always at hand, a distraction.

After Rogers had been in business for about ten years, he put a gumshoe on the payroll. He was the first big-time lawyer to employ a detective for investigating hostile witnesses—and jurors. The dick, a red-faced, whisky-breathing man of sixty, named Callahan, had formerly worked on the Los Angeles Police Department and probably knew where more bodies were buried than any man in Los Angeles. Moreover, Callahan had pipelines into the district attorney's office. When a case came in to Rogers, Callahan had standing instructions not only to find out who the state's principal witnesses would be but to locate the skeletons in their closets so that Earl could discredit their testimony.

Callahan's first important job for Rogers came when Earl was retained by a prominent society man to defend him on a charge of having caused the death of a girl while seducing her. The state's principal witness was to be an obscure physician who was all set to tell a jury that the girl had died of injuries sustained because of the physical dimensions of the man.

"Look into this doctor," Rogers told Callahan. "See what you can dig up about him."

At the trial, after the doctor had given his testimony, Rogers got up to cross-examine. Holding a book in his hand, he asked the witness whether there was the slightest doubt in his mind about the physical-dimension aspect of the case, that this had caused the fatal injuries.

"No doubt of it."

"You have always thought so, Doctor?"

"Always."

Riffling through the book, Rogers found a certain page and for a moment read to himself. "But Doctor," he continued, "it says in this medical book that there is no case on record where a man's size has brought about a fatality." He held up the book —too far from the witness for the physician to read the title. "What do you say to that?"

"Bosh," said the doctor. "That book cannot be accurate. It can have no scientific basis."

"But this book is *authoritative*, Doctor," Rogers insisted, "and it absolutely contradicts your testimony."

The prosecutor leaped to his feet demanding to know who had written the book.

"Why," said Rogers, jerking his head in the direction of the physician, "the state's expert witness here wrote it."

While the prosecutor and the witness stewed in their own juices, Rogers turned to the jury, raised his eyebrows, and snapped, "That will be all, *Doc*-tor."

When, in 1910, Earl Rogers reached his fortieth birthday, he happened to pick up a novel that was to influence his life considerably. The book, called *The Right of Way*, by Sir Gilbert Parker, was the story of a character called Charley (Beauty) Steele, a colorful Montreal lawyer. Steele was described as a devastatingly handsome dog, a great dresser, a great drinker, and a great lover.

Rogers decided that Beauty Steele was the most fascinating hero he had ever read about. By the time he laid down the volume, he had arrived at an important decision. Thereafter, he would be as much like Steele as possible. He'd begin to act a part and bring to life a totally fictional character.

Steele was a bitter cynic. Earl, already cynical, grew more so.

Steele, the dandy dresser, became Earl's model in clothes. Earl began to affect spats, Ascot ties, and top coats with fur collars —an incongruous costume for Southern California. Steele sported a monocle. Earl tried one, but settled instead for a lorgnette—fashionable then for both men and women.

It was in the beginning of the Charley Steele phase that Earl moved his family from Los Angeles to a comfortable house in Hollywood. The future movie capital was still only a sparse region of lemon groves, with the flicker industry having hardly more than a foothold.

And it was at about the same time that Earl's marriage to Hazel Belle really began to come apart at the seams. One night Earl was reading in his study at home, a highball at his side, when his wife entered.

"Earl," she said, "we've been married seventeen years."

"So we have," said Rogers, not lifting his eyes from the book.

"In all that time," she went on, "you've seldom taken me out."

"No," Rogers admitted, "I haven't."

"How long do you expect a woman to stand for that, Earl? How do you think I like it when people tell me they've seen you around with other women enjoying yourself, while I stay home taking care of the children?"

Rogers laid down his book. "Who's been carrying tales?" he asked.

"It makes no difference. I know that there are other women— that there have been all along, practically since the beginning."

"Well, why haven't you said anything about it before?"

Mrs. Rogers drew a deep breath. "I wanted to keep our marriage together for the sake of the children. I hoped you would change. You never will."

"No," said Rogers, "I guess I won't." He looked at his wife

as he would at a witness he was about to cross-examine. "What do you intend to do about it?"

"I want a divorce."

"Oh?"

"I know your pride is hurt, Earl, but a divorce is the best thing. Maybe you'll find somebody else you'll think enough of to stop this awful drinking."

"You've never complained about my drinking before."

"No. I suppose I thought you might change about that, too. But you'll never stop for me."

"No, I guess I won't, at that." He looked at his glass. It was empty. He went out to the kitchen to fill it. When he came back and sat down again, the glass at his lips, his wife said, "Well, Earl, what about the divorce?"

"All right," he said. "I'll give you one on grounds of cruelty. How much money do you want?"

"I'd like this house. It's all paid for. It's all we have. You spend everything else. So I want the house and three hundred dollars a month and the children."

Rogers looked hard at his wife as he considered the terms. "All right," he said. "I'll arrange it."

The divorce went through. Earl Rogers moved to a bachelor's apartment in suburban Ocean Park and began stocking the place with liquor and women.

Not long after, a moon-faced young fellow walked into Earl's office suite and demanded to see him. Earl was nursing a painful hangover and had told his secretary he wanted no visitors. But the moon-faced lad was insistent. He became so highly vocal about it that the grouchy Rogers emerged from his private office to see what all the fuss was about.

Moonface turned out to be a collection agent who had come to dun Rogers into paying up for a set of books. Earl—even though at the moment he hated the world—liked the boy's appearance and personality, and he soon detected a hot-shot mind. Questioning him, he found the lad was paying for a law course with this part-time job. Rogers made a fast decision.

"How'd you like to study law in my office?" he asked.

The boy's eyes widened. "Do you really mean that?"

"You bet I do. I think you'll make a great lawyer."

And that's how Jerry Geisler, today the best-known lawyer in the Golden State, got his start. Geisler, who never succeeded in collecting for Earl's books, was to become associated with him in many of Earl's most important cases. Jerry's great value was his uncanny ability to anticipate what the opposition's strategy would be. Sometimes, before a trial even got under way, he prepared an outline of the tactics he foresaw and usually hit the plan right on the button.

A much more famous figure of the time, however, got associated with Rogers in a far different way. Earl was checking into his office about 11 o'clock one morning when he gave a double take at a small, unkempt, scowling middle-aged figure sitting in the waiting room.

"Why," said Earl, approaching and extending his hand, "you must be Clarence Darrow."

"I am," said the great lawyer of Chicago. "I thought I'd drop in on you. My wife and I were in court yesterday when you got an acquittal for that confidence man. Now I'd like you to defend me."

"I'll be glad to, Mr. Darrow. You flatter me by choosing me as your counsel."

"I suppose you know all about my case."

"In a general way," said Rogers, "from reading the papers."

William J. Burns, the country's number-one detective of the era, who enjoyed a reputation similar to that of J. Edgar Hoover today, had constructed a juror-bribing case against Darrow. It orginated in the trial of the notorious McNamara brothers who, in a labor war, had dynamited the open-shop *Los Angeles Times* for a toll of twenty-one lives. Darrow conducted the defense. But after the trial was over, a juror named Lockwood claimed he had been approached by an investigator for Darrow called Franklin and offered five thousand dollars to hold out against conviction. Lockwood not only voted with the other jurors to convict the brothers but complained to William J. Burns, who had investigated the *Times* explosion and trapped the McNamaras. Burns put the screws to Darrow's man, and Franklin, confessing the whole plot, declared the bribe offer was Darrow's idea.

Earl Rogers' problem, therefore, was to extricate Darrow from the net of evidence that Lockwood, Franklin, and Burns were all set to weave around him.

When the trial began, the prosecutor, John D. Fredericks, a wily adversary, made a production of examining each prospective juror before accepting him. Rogers was quick to turn Fredericks' tactics to advantage. He asked none of the jurors a thing. After Fredericks had quizzed a man on everything he could think of, Rogers would smile and say, "No questions," then, turning to the judge, add, "I find this gentleman infinitely acceptable."

Darrow, sitting there rubbing the stubble on his chin, looked on Rogers' performance with jaundiced eyes. After the sixth juror was accepted, he whispered, "Why the hell don't you ask them *some* questions?"

"The prosecutor is asking so many," Rogers answered, "that I'm making friends by asking none."

Lockwood told his story of the bribe attempt simply and convincingly.

"No questions," said Rogers.

The strategy surprised Darrow, who was so worried he wasn't thinking clearly. "Why didn't you cross-examine him?" he whispered.

"He made too good an impression on the jury," Rogers replied.

Franklin, the Darrow investigator who had spilled the beans to Burns, was a scurvy-looking character. When it came time for his cross-examination, Earl stepped up close to the witness stand, whipped out his lorgnette and stared. When Franklin began to look a little uneasy, Rogers turned and faced the jury.

"Isn't it a fact, Mr. Franklin," he began, "that you have been in the pay of the district attorney right along and offered your services to Mr. Darrow merely to trump up this false charge?"

Prosecutor Fredericks leaped to his feet howling an objection. Rogers whipped out the lorgnette, tilted his head, and eyed his opponent in surprise. The judge instructed Rogers to abandon that line of questioning.

"Very well," Rogers agreed, and addressed the witness again. "Isn't it a fact that you were, under the assumed name of"— here Rogers consulted a piece of paper that was completely blank—"under the assumed name of Wentworth Harwood, convicted of perjury in the state of Illinois in"—again he consulted the blank paper—"the year of 1904?"

"Of course not!" screamed the witness.

"My mistake," said Rogers. "I mean 1905."

"Certainly not!"

Rogers smiled. "1906, then?" No!

"1907?"

The prosecutor objected bitterly, but Rogers kept on slyly assaulting Franklin with queries that, however unfounded, cast serious doubt on his integrity. Such questioning would not be allowed now, but in those days practically anything went.

When he was through with Franklin, Rogers whispered to Darrow he had pretty well convinced the jury that the witness was a liar, a perjurer, a swindler, a con man, and a fugitive from justice.

Then it came time for Rogers to cross-examine William J. Burns. The detective, with his natty attire, snapping blue eyes, steel-trap mind, and air of painful integrity, was ruffled by the way Rogers peered at him. Once when Earl gave Billy the lorgnette treatment Burns almost blew a fuse. Turning to the judge, he demanded, "Your Honor, make this man stop looking at me as if I were an—an *insect!*"

One morning Burns appeared in court carrying a fancy cane.

"I can make use of that cane," Rogers whispered.

"How?" asked Darrow.

"I'm going to make him lift it. Then I'll accuse him of threatening me."

Rogers began to quiz Burns about his integrity—something of which the founder of the Burns International Detective Agency was mighty proud. Earl had learned that all a man had to do to drive Burns to the verge of apoplexy was to ask him if he had ever been accused of a dishonest act. He asked the question.

"No!" roared Burns.

"Well," continued Rogers, "have you ever been accused of an *unethical* act—one that was not honest but not quite dishonest?"

"No, I have not," roared the witness, "and that's more than you can say!"

Rogers knew Burns had him there. That one remark, in fact, set Rogers and Darrow back nearly all they had gained.

Now Rogers, who had been standing some distance from the detective, slowly stepped forward until he was practically breathing in Burns' face. The nearness of the lawyer caused Burns to shift in his seat, and as he did so, he lifted the cane in the air.

Rogers took a quick hard look at the cane, cringed, placed his hands in front of his eyes, and backed away.

"Your Honor!" he yelled. "The witness has a *sword* in that cane!"

Burns was flabbergasted.

"Make him open up that cane, Your Honor!" cried Rogers, still holding one hand over his face and pointing to Burns with the other. "Make him take out the sword and give it to the bailiff."

Burns, his jaw hanging loose, handed the cane to the court officer. "Examine it all you want," he said. "There's no sword in there."

"My mistake," said Rogers. "But he does carry a sword in a cane that looks just like this one."

"You're a liar!" Burns barked.

Rogers looked deeply hurt.

During the balance of the cross-examination, Rogers acted like a man fearful of physical attack. This air made Burns madder and madder—which only induced Rogers to look still more scared.

As the trial progressed, Rogers saw to it that the prosecutor was constantly objecting to his line of questioning and that the judge was always bawling him out. Consequently, by the time he rose to make his summation he had managed to place himself, rather than Darrow, on trial.

And then Rogers, too hungover for a long summation, made it brief.

"Gentlemen," he said to the jurors, "I ask you merely to answer for yourselves a question of simple logic. Does it make sense to suppose that Mr. Darrow, who has spent so many years building up his reputation as the country's greatest lawyer, would place that reputation, and his whole career, in jeopardy by going to a perfect stranger and saying, 'Here's some money. Go out and buy me a juror. I trust you absolutely. I trust you never to divulge a thing about this transaction between you and me.' Gentlemen, does that make sense?"

The way Rogers asked the question, the expression on his face, the tone of his voice, the very way he stood, made the state's entire case sound utterly ridiculous.

And now Darrow personally took over the summation, and he was at his dramatic best. Dwelling more on the long history of his life rather than on the issue at bar, he talked on and on, pulling out all the stops. When he had finished telling the jurors, in effect, what a prince among men he really was, there was hardly a dry eye in the courtroom, in or out of the jury box.

The jury acquitted Clarence Darrow.

Earl Rogers' talent for downright sharpness emerged in a cold light in his handling the defense of a character known around the Los Angeles area as Mad Mike Melrose. Mad Mike was the postmaster of Acton, a ranching town near Los Angeles. A belligerent citizen, he had had words several times with rancher Billy Broome.

One scorching midsummer day, several shots were fired in front of the Acton post office. When the smoke cleared away, Broome, who had been wearing only a pair of pants, was lying in the street dead and Mad Mike Melrose was standing over him. The rancher had apparently been unarmed because when the sheriff arrived there was only one gun around—the empty weapon in the hand of Melrose.

There was just one eye-witness to the scene—a man named Phillips, who had been standing inside the post office and rushed outside when he heard the first shot. He saw Broome lying face down on the ground and Melrose leaning over him, holding his gun against the rancher's bare back and firing away.

There it was, an open-and-shut case: a nasty character who had quarreled with another man was seen giving him the business. Melrose, from his jail cell, uttered an anguished cry for Earl Rogers.

The first thing Rogers did was to get his gumshoe, Callahan, climbing his pipeline into the district attorney's office. Callahan learned that the slain man had been buried without anyone's having noticed whether or not there were powder marks on the back of the corpse.

Earl's next move was clear. He would have to open the grave of the murdered man. So, one dark night Rogers and a couple of laborers went to the cemetery where the rancher was buried. Earl acted as look-out while the two laborers dug down. When they reached Broome's coffin, they pried it open.

Then, as the laborers came out, Rogers went into the grave with a lantern. He turned the body over on its side and pulled up its shirt and coat. Sure enough, there were powder burns on the back.

Rogers had come prepared. He took a bottle of acid out of his pocket and poured the contents over the burns. Then he carefully rearranged the corpse, closed the casket, and climbed out. His two helpers replaced the dirt, and the three slunk away.

When the murder trial opened, Phillips, the witness, told his story in a perfectly straightforward manner. Starting his cross-examination, Rogers summoned one of his staff and asked the man to strip to the waist.

"Now," he said, "lie down on the floor in front of the jury box."

Then Earl called Phillips down from the witness stand and gave his instructions.

"Just show His Honor and the gentlemen of the jury how poor Broome was lying when, as you say, the defendant shot him several times in the back."

After arranging the "corpse" face down, Phillips asked, "What now?"

Rogers handed the witness a revolver. "Don't be afraid," he said. "It's not loaded. Now just lean down and show me exactly how close you say the defendant held the gun to Broome's bare back when the shots were fired."

Phillips shoved the gun right against the subject's back.

"You mean," Rogers demanded, "the gun was touching Broome, or practically touching him, when you saw those shots fired?"

"Yes, sir."

"*Sure* of that?"

"Yes, sir."

"Abso*lute*ly?"

"Yes, sir."

Rogers turned to the prosecutor. "I presume," he said, "that you are prepared to offer testimony showing that the skin on the back of the slain man bore *powder burns*."

The D. A. coughed. "Well," he said, "not exactly."

"What!" Rogers exclaimed. "You mean to stand there, sir, and say you are not prepared to produce evidence of powder burns—the burns that most certainly would have been on the back of the corpse if this witness"—Rogers waved contemptuously toward Phillips—"is telling the *truth?*"

The D. A. had to admit that he had no such evidence.

The result: disagreement.

For the second trial the prosecutor opened up Broome's grave to get the information he had overlooked. Earl Rogers' acid had done its work well. The skin and part of the flesh on Broome's back was eaten away. The D. A. had his suspicions, but there was nothing he could prove.

At the trial Rogers introduced new evidence to indicate that Broome had shot several times at Melrose and Mad Mike had simply acted in self-defense. This was news to the district attorney, because nobody had mentioned previously that Broome had a gun. But Earl had found a man willing to testify he had sold the rancher a rifle.

"And now," said Rogers, "will the court attendant please bring in the tree in the corridor so the jury can get a good look at it?"

A small tree was dragged in, and Rogers pointed out several bullet holes in its trunk. Then he produced the spent bullets which he claimed he had dug out of the trunk. They were the same caliber as the rifle that Rogers' witness said he had sold.

"My client here kept telling me that Broome emptied his gun at him," Rogers explained. "As fortune would have it, we found the weapon."

The gun, he said, had been secreted in a clump of bushes near the scene of the shooting. "Probably by some friend of Broome's—or an enemy of the defendant." Naturally, Rogers went on, when he located the gun he renewed his search for some trace of the bullets fired at his client—and found the tree.

Another hung jury.

Melrose went on trial a third time. Still another hung jury—but this one was ten to two for *acquittal*. Finally the case against Melrose was dropped.

One of the most arresting figures banging around Los Angeles when Earl Rogers was in his heyday was a drunken, eccentric multimillionaire by the name of Griffith Griffith. Griffith had an over-sized head, a fat pot, and spindly legs, adding up to the appearance of a gnome. He and Rogers used to drink at the same bars, and while they never became close friends, they enjoyed an alcoholic acquaintance.

Rogers knew the millionaire, who had collected his money in mining and realty, would be in serious trouble sooner or later. More important, the old boy would be in a position to pay handsomely to get out.

One candidate for making trouble was Griffith's wife, a very religious woman. Her rich husband suffered from the delusion that she and practically all the churches of the world were in a plot to pry his millions away from him. To forestall this possibility, Griffith became a philanthropist. He donated to the City of Los Angeles land for a huge park bearing his name, and he underwrote the construction of Griffith Observatory, one of the world's foremost star-gazing plants.

One day when he and his wife were spending a quarrelsome holiday at Santa Monica, the millionaire got a little more tanked up than usual. Whipping out a gun in their hotel suite, he told his wife to start praying.

"What for?" she asked, not believing her eyes.

"Because I'm going to kill you for plotting to get my money."

Griffith fired a single shot. It was not fatal, but it did blind his wife in one eye. When he was clapped in jail, he remembered Earl Rogers and sent for him.

Earl concluded that the only defense a jury would swallow was that Griffith was insane from drink. This was to be the first time in California that the defendant in a major trial would attempt to escape through such a plea.

During the trial, Rogers had Griffith act as nutty as a fruitcake. Earl's principal witness was Dr. H. M. Butler, head of the Los Angeles branch of the Keeley Cure Institute.

"Doctor," Rogers began, "you of the Keeley Cure are authorities on the effects of alcohol on the human body. Would you be kind enough to explain to the jury just how my client became insane through over-indulgence in strong drink—how, in fact, he was not responsible for his actions?"

"I'd be glad to," said the physician. He thereupon gave the jurors a fascinating lecture on what excessive drink does to the human brain and the human emotions. By the time Dr. Butler was through, he seemed to have sold a couple of jurors on indicting the state of California for putting a poor old drunk on trial just because he had shot out his wife's eye.

Rogers was out in the corridor smoking when the jury sent word that it had reached a verdict.

"What do you think it'll be, Earl?" asked a reporter.

"Acquittal of course," answered Rogers.

But it wasn't an acquittal. It was a conviction, recommending leniency. The judge sentenced Griffith to two years.

The opinion around town soon developed that Rogers had got Griffith off lightly. But the verdict plunged Earl into the depths of depression. Feeling he was slipping, he went on an alcoholic marathon and was gone for two weeks.

Earl's favorite hangout was the Ship Cafe in Venice, down the coast from Hollywood. The Ship Cafe was the glamor spot of the Los Angeles area, a stamping ground of Hollywood stars and directors when they were relaxing.

Rogers was in the Ship one night alone, eating well and drinking better. At the next table were two attractive girls and their escort. The younger of the girls—in her twenties, with wind-blown hair, saucer eyes, and a rosebud mouth—kept glancing at Earl. He pretended not to notice. Instead, he made quite a production of sending his food back as unsatisfactory.

Finally he heard her whisper, "Who is that interesting man?"

The escort shook his head. "You don't want anything to do with him. That's Earl Rogers, the crooked lawyer."

"Never heard of him," said the girl. "But I'd like to meet him."

Earl got up and made his way over. He bowed to the girls, then turned to their escort.

"I think it is presumptuous of you, sir," he said, "to try to poison the mind of this charming young lady against me. I'll thank you to keep your opinions to yourself." Then he lifted the right hand of the girl and brushed it with his lips. "Charmed," he murmured, "utterly charmed."

The girl's name was Edna Landers, called Teddy. She was from the Middle West and had come to Los Angeles with her sister to study voice. Sister, it turned out, was unhappily married and was shopping around for a divorce lawyer. Earl decided on the spot that there was one sure way to get to know Teddy better. He took her sister's case for peanuts.

While the divorce mill was grinding, Earl began to squire Teddy around town. Being some twenty years younger, she was practically hypnotized by him. Headwaiters bowed deeply to him, and taxi drivers shouted greetings as he and Teddy strolled along the streets of downtown Los Angeles. When the two sat at ringside at the fights, both fighters and referees leaned over the ropes to pay their respects.

Earl and Teddy were at the Pacific Athletic Club one night when the two heavyweights who were to slug it out in the main event entered the ring. One of them—Bull Young—drew Earl's attention. Using his medical knowledge, Earl studied the fighter intently.

"There's something wrong with Young," he said to Teddy. "He doesn't look like a man who ought to be fighting."

Young was knocked out in the eleventh round. While the referee was counting, Earl said, "Young isn't going to get up."

Young didn't. He died in a hospital a few hours later without regaining consciousness.

Rogers was never an ambulance chaser, but when Young's opponent was arrested and charged with manslaughter, Earl went to his cell.

"I'll take your case," he said, "and you needn't worry about money. A thing like this could ruin you if it's not handled right."

Earl went to the medical examiner and demanded to know the cause of Young's death. The examiner thought the fighter's brain had been damaged.

"Well," said Earl, "open up his head and prove it. Another man's future is at stake."

Young's head was opened up, but it didn't yield the cause of death. Suspicious, Earl began to investigate the doctor who okayed fighters for the club. He learned that the sawbones didn't give them much of an examination, and when he did, didn't put much stock in what he found. Earl confronted the doctor and took a long chance.

"Why," he asked, "didn't you put a stop to this fight when you found Young had a bad heart?"

"How do you know he had a bad heart?"

"Never mind about that. Why didn't you prevent the fight?"

The doctor shrugged. "I didn't think his heart condition was that serious. It didn't seem to be anything to stop the fight for."

"Exactly what did you hear when you listened to Young's heart?"

"Just a slight irregularity."

"All right," said Rogers. "You're coming with me to tell about it."

The manslaughter charge against Young's opponent was dropped.

"You're a great fighter," Earl said to his client. "Some day you might be heavyweight champ."

Rogers couldn't have been more right. For his client was Jess Willard, who, not long afterward, took the heavyweight crown from Jack Johnson at Havana.

One day Earl and Teddy went to the races at Santa Anita. Teddy had never been at a track before, and that particular day there was to be run an event called the Earl Rogers Handicap. She was suitably impressed.

"Gosh," she said simply, "you sure are important. Why, some day you could be governor, maybe even President. If only you didn't drink so much."

While the handicap was being run, Earl forgot the horses. He was looking at Teddy. He had been taking her around for three months now, and he hadn't even tried to kiss her. It seemed so satisfactory just to be in her company that he had even stopped seeing other women. As he sat there looking at her, it came to him that he was in love. At forty-five he was as happy as a schoolboy of seventeen.

When the race was over, he took Teddy by the hand.

"Teddy," he said, in his rich voice, "I want to marry you. I don't want to live without you. Let's be married right away."

She turned away a moment, then back directly to him. "I'll marry you, Earl," she said, "on one condition."

"That I stop drinking?"

She nodded.

He raised his free hand. "I swear," he said, "I'll never touch another drop as long as there is life in me."

He leaned over and kissed her—and when the cheers went up they realized that everyone around was watching. Someone shouted, "When's the wedding, Earl?"

Rogers grinned and called back, "As soon as we can find a preacher."

Earl Rogers was a changed man after he married Teddy Landers. They moved into a little house in the Hollywood hills. Earl was really on the wagon, and he never looked at another woman. His sole vice seemed to be smoking about four packs a day of his brown cigarettes. He remained friendly with his ex-wife, and Teddy saw to it that he paid her the three hundred dollars a month he had promised. The children were now in their teens and often visited Earl and Teddy, seeing, in fact, more of their father than they ever had.

Earl's former drinking cronies saw him only if they went to his trials. When an acquittal verdict came in and Earl walked out of the courtroom with his briefcase, the old friends would be hanging around in the corridor, hoping he would join them for a night of it.

"I'm a changed man, boys," Earl said each time, smiling. "None of the old life for me ever again."

Teddy used to attend most of Earl's trials. Sitting in the front row, she looked on admiringly as he wove his magic on witnesses and jurors. Every once in a while, when he had done something particularly clever, he turned around, caught her eye, and said, simply by raising an eyebrow, "How am I doing?"

Financially, Earl was doing all right. Now, when the fees came in, he handed them over to Teddy and she banked them— in her name.

The fact that Earl Rogers knew so much about so many people around Los Angeles was one of the keys to his continuing success in the courtroom. His friendship with Spike McAllister was a case in point.

McAllister and Rogers had been barroom cronies. McAllister, a big hunk of man, was a lady killer. Although a mining engineer by profession, he devoted most of his time to prospecting for blondes. The result was that he was usually broke, and being broke he borrowed money from women instead of paying them.

McAllister could see out of only one eye. He had lost the sight of the other—his right—through illness, years before coming to Los Angeles. Nobody but a few close friends, however, among them Rogers, knew that.

For some time McAllister had been living with a wealthy widow in her home as a paid guest. He was given bed and board, in that order, and fifty dollars a week. It was a nice arrangement, for a man who could face himself.

One morning McAllister and the widow got into an argument and McAllister shot her dead. He'd hardly dropped the gun before he was phoning Earl Rogers.

"Earl," he said, "I just shot the old bag. What'll I do?"

"Did anybody hear the shooting?" asked Rogers.

"I don't think so."

"All right," said Earl. "Don't open the door to anybody until I get there. I'll knock six times."

Rogers thought things over briefly and called in Callahan.

"I want you to buy some nitric acid," he said. "Take a cab and go somewhere you won't be recognized. If the druggist asks what you want it for, tell him you're a chemist and you need it for an experiment."

With the bottle of acid in his pocket, Rogers walked into the murder house and studied the corpse.

"Now listen closely, Mac," he said. "It was still dark, just before daylight, and you got up to investigate a noise. You had this gun on a night table and you took it for self-protection. You were no sooner out of bed than somebody threw acid in your face. You almost went out of your mind with the pain and you fired the gun involuntarily. Then you fell unconscious. When you woke up you found you had killed this woman."

"But nobody threw any acid at me," said McAllister.

"I'm going to, Mac. I'm going to throw it in that right eye of yours. You can claim the acid blinded that eye and you didn't know who you were firing at. Then you'll have to have the eye removed. That won't make any difference in your sight."

Before McAllister could grasp the import of the lawyer's strategy, Earl threw the acid at the right side of his client's face. McAllister started to scream with pain.

"Keep your voice down, Mac," said Rogers, "until I get out of here. Then call the police."

After the jury acquitted him, Spike McAllister went out and bought a glass eye.

With verdicts like this coming in, everything was going just fine for Earl Rogers. And then, in 1918, he suddenly seemed to realize he was not far from his fiftieth birthday. His home life with Teddy couldn't have been happier. Because she handled his money so well, for the first time in his life, he could pay his bills on time. He went to church practically every Sunday. He had even turned down some murder cases in order to take on more respectable civil suits. And he hadn't touched a drop of liquor since that day at Santa Anita when he had promised Teddy to swear off.

But now he was nearly fifty—and restless. He remembered the old life—the good liquor and the laughs with the boys— and he grew irritable at the thought of never having any of it. Teddy sensed the change quickly.

"Aren't you happy with me any more, Earl?" she asked him one night.

"Certainly," he said. "But a man feels like breaking loose once in a while."

Next afternoon he phoned Teddy from the office. "I won't be home until late," he said. "Something has come up."

"All right," said Teddy. "I'll wait up for you."

"No," he said sharply, "don't do that."

But Teddy did wait. She waited all night. In the morning she went to his office and sat there till past noon.

It was then that a policeman came in. Earl had been picked up in a gutter and the cops had taken him to a station house to sleep it off.

Teddy was there at the station house when Earl woke up. She made it short and sweet.

"Earl," she said, "it's been wonderful while it lasted. But now we're through."

"But this is the only time I've ever fallen off the wagon," he protested. "Give me another chance."

Teddy had an icy streak. "There would only be another chance after that, Earl, and another after *that*. It would never end. If you want liquor now, after how happy we've been, you'll always want it."

Earl pleaded desperately, but it was no dice. "I'll send you all the money I've saved for you," she said, and got ready to go.

"For heaven's sake don't do that!" he cried. "That's your money."

"Well, then, I'll see that if anything happens to me your children will get it."

Teddy beat Earl back to their home and packed her things. By the time he got there she had gone, and when he tried to find her, he couldn't. She had learned from him how to hide out.

Rogers now hit the bottle in earnest and became more drunk than sober. Loyal Jerry Geisler tried to help him. But Earl was too much, and Jerry finally had to give up and go into business for himself.

Earl left his house in Hollywood and took a little place in suburban Ocean Park. He was there in bed at noon on a February day of 1919, a few months after Teddy had left him, when his daughter Adela walked in.

"Get dressed, Dad," she said, "and come with me. Teddy's in a hospital in Los Angeles. She's very ill with influenza and wants you."

Rogers got dressed and jumped into Adela's car. The car broke down on a lonely stretch of road a few minutes after they started. It took more than an hour to get a taxi.

When Earl reached the hospital he rushed in and asked for Teddy's room. The nurse at the desk looked up at him gently.

"I'm very sorry, Mr. Rogers," she said. "Your wife died a few minutes ago."

From that day on, Earl Rogers tried to commit suicide with the bottle. There were only brief periods when he sobered up enough to take a case, and business fell off to practically nothing.

Rogers had just passed his fiftieth birthday when he made his next-to-last appearance in a major trial. He was defending a wealthy young man by the name of Haines, who was accused of having illegally escaped the draft in the First World War. Uncle Sam alleged that Haines had gone to a professional nurse who was a bird dog for a highly specialized optometrist. The eye man made glasses that deteriorated rather than improved the sight of wealthy cowards. With Haines the nurse and the optometrist were also being tried, although each had separate counsel.

The morning the trial began, Rogers was late for the opening of court. When he did show up, the judge and the courtroom attachés gave him a triple take. Rogers was half plastered. He had several days' beard on his face. He had slept in his suit, and it looked it, and his collar and shirt cuffs were dirty. He looked up at the judge, who had known him in his better days, like a dog waiting to get in out of the cold.

"Perhaps counsel is not feeling well," said His Honor, "and would like to be excused. Perhaps counsel for one of the other defendants would like to substitute for Mr. Rogers."

"No, Your Honor," Rogers mumbled. "I'll be all right."

Rogers was far from all right. He sat with his chin on his chest, practically asleep, while the jury was chosen. Nor did he wake up much when the prosecution began its case against Rogers' client and the co-defendants—and a damning case it was, too.

When it came Earl's turn to put his client on the stand, he looked more like a sleepwalker than a defense counsel. His questions were mechanical. And when he had finished, he went back to his chair and slumped over. While he was dozing, the prosecutor practically crucified Haines in cross-examination.

Then came the morning when Rogers was to appear before the jury and make his closing address. He was not present when court opened. His Honor glanced toward Rogers' empty seat.

"Where," he asked the attorneys for the two others on trial, "is counsel for the defendant Haines?" The other lawyers didn't know.

Then in the rear of the courtroom there was a slight commotion. Earl Rogers had arrived—a different Rogers from the bum who had been dozing since the trial began. Here was the old Earl Rogers. Overnight the bum had changed back to an alert, beautifully turned-out gentleman. His suit was clean and pressed, his hair slicked back, his linen immaculate. Freshly barbered and bathed, he gave off a faint scent of perfume.

He stood in the back of the courtroom just inside the doors, like an actor making an entrance—which he very well knew. Reaching into his pocket, he pulled out the famous lorgnette and examined the spectators.

Apparently satisfied that every eye was on him, he lowered the glass and strode smartly to the bench. Bowing to the judge, he smiled and apologized for his tardiness. His Honor, impressed by the transformation, said, "That's quite all right, Mr. Rogers."

And now the great Earl Rogers of years past began his summation. He turned toward the center of the jury box. His expression grave, he peered into the face of each juror. Then he bowed his head for a moment, lost in thought. When he raised it again, he spoke.

"Gentlemen," he said, "you are about to pass judgment on my client. You are about to decide whether this charge—this charge of the great government of the United States that the young man before you willfully avoided the draft by deliberately damaging his eyes—is true or false. I might say at the very outset, gentlemen, that if there is the slightest suspicion in your minds there is so much as a shred of truth in this charge, by all means bring in a verdict of guilty."

Rogers began to pace up and down, the supreme courtroom actor of the golden days, the slinking, deadly adversary. At one end of the jury box, with his back to the judge, he looked above the heads of the jurors, off into space. He smiled faintly, as if in apology, and then he began to speak again. He started with his own background. His grandfather had been a great patriot, and his father as well. And his eldest son was in their company.

"My own boy," he said. "What did my own boy do when he

heard the call to the colors? Why, gentlemen, he went out and enlisted. Nothing, thank God, was wrong with his eyesight."

But if something had been wrong with the boy's sight, Earl continued, did the jurors know what he would have done? Precisely what the defendant did. He would have gone to an eye specialist to correct his sight, so that he could still defend his country. Was it the fault of the defendant, therefore, that the optometrist had given him a pair of injurious glasses?

The jury convicted both the optometrist and the nurse. But it brought in an acquittal for Rogers' client.

"Now," Earl told the youth, "go out and get your eyes fixed up and join the Army. *I'm* going out and get good and drunk."

Rogers had no sooner recovered from the debauch that followed than he was approached by relatives of Harold Denham, a soldier who was being held for killing a Los Angeles grocer during a hold-up.

Rogers took the case simply because he needed the money. But, after examining the facts, he decided that Denham didn't have much of a chance. So he went to the district attorney and offered to plead his boy guilty to second-degree murder. The D. A. said nothing doing.

"All right," said Rogers, "I'll plead him guilty to first degree if you can fix it up so he will get life instead of the gallows."

"No, Earl," said the D. A. "We've got too good a case on this fellow. We want to make an example of him. We want to show the public that soldiers can't come here and get drunk and kill people and get away with it.

At Denham's trial, Rogers staked everything on his old magic with a jury.

"Gentlemen," he said, when he went into his summation, "there is no question that my client killed this poor grocer during a hold-up. But consider this: Here was a boy who had been trained in the art of killing—a boy who was told by his own government that human life meant nothing and that he was shortly to be sent over the ocean to make a career of taking human life.

"Now, gentlemen," Rogers went on, standing stock still, with a holy light in his eyes, "what could we expect a boy thus trained to do, when already under the influence of drink he wanted money for more? Only what he did, wrong as it was. This boy is a victim of circumstances, a product of this strange era in which we live." Rogers stopped to allow his words to sink in. "Do you know who should be on trial here, gentlemen? Not this boy, certainly. His government—the government of the United States—is the one who is responsible for this heinous murder. I leave you with that thought."

Rogers went back to his seat and held his head in his hands.

The jury wasn't out very long. When it came in, it handed up a verdict of death on the gallows for Harold Denham. Rogers cocked an ear toward the foreman of the jury.

"May I ask the foreman to repeat that verdict," he said, as if he didn't trust his ears.

"Murder in the first degree," said the foreman, "with no recommendation for mercy."

Rogers shot a glance at the D.A. who had refused to make a deal with him. "I hope you're satisfied," he said. "I hope you can sleep tonight after sending this boy to his death."

Rogers clapped on his hat and hurried from the courtroom. When he was picked up in a gutter a few days later, his family had him committed to an institution on the outskirts of Los Angeles. Earl was too weak to resist.

After he'd been released from the cure, Earl went right back to drinking again. He took a hole-in-the-wall office in a rundown building and had his name painted on the door.

Only a year had passed since the death of Teddy, and Earl was down at the heels and frayed at the cuffs. He hit one stretch where he didn't have a dime. He was ejected from his shabby little office for non-payment of rent, and the only room he could find was in a cheap lodging house on the edge of Chinatown.

One day in February, 1921, Earl Rogers sank into a chair in the lodging house and gazed steadily at the calendar behind the desk. Finally he spoke.

"Do you know," he said to the clerk, "it was just three years ago today that I lost the only woman I ever loved. Three years ago today exactly." He was silent for a moment. "Can you lend me a quarter for a drink?" he asked.

The clerk held out the coin, and Rogers shuffled out into the sunshine. In a little while he was back.

"Did you get your drink?" asked the clerk.

Rogers nodded but didn't speak. He dropped into a chair and stared at the wall. His head slumped over on his chest.

"That must have been a powerful drink," said the clerk.

Earl Rogers didn't answer. He just sat there for more than two hours. Then it occurred to the clerk that he was very still, even for a drunk.

Earl Rogers was dead.

CLARENCE DARROW

The old Criminal Courts Building in Chicago was the habitat of the greatest aggregation of hard-drinking reporters, assorted malefactors, shyster lawyers, heartless prosecutors, and book-throwing judges ever assembled in one American legal arena. It is difficult, in retrospect, to point the finger at the most colorful performer in the all-star cast. Some spectators to the show would choose Hildy Johnson, the old Hearst reporter (the central character in the play *The Front Page*) who one day hid an escaped murderer in his roll-top desk in the pressroom. But when it comes to nominating the most colorful lawyer ever to gain acquittals for murderers, pickpockets, second-story specialists, dippers into the public till, madams of brothels and their horizontal merchandise, it is Clarence Seward Darrow, hands down.

Darrow was the master courtroom strategist. Although he was accused only once of jury bribing during more than half a century of trial work, he was so adept at smelling out legal loopholes, clothing guilty clients in the garments of innocence, and mesmerizing juries, that he accomplished more, with a legal framework, than mouthpieces who were out-and-out crooks. Darrow was a staunch advocate of that legal tenet that holds that a man is innocent until proved guilty. Although he often knew in his own mind that a client was dripping with guilt, he felt justified in pulling all the legal levers to gain an acquittal. It was his conviction that the law was an imperfect instrument. The forces that drove a man to murder or to theft, or a woman to shoplifting or prostitution, were, to Darrow's mind, a bewildering mixture of heredity and environment—far beyond the comprehension of the average judge or jury. Who, then, was to say that this man should go to the gallows, or that this woman should go to the workhouse?

As a boy in a small Ohio town, Clarence Darrow had seen innocent men convicted of offenses they had never committed because they did not have proper legal representation—and he had never forgotten it. As a man, he knew of cases where mitigating circumstances should have gotten killers off with prison terms or even acquittals, rather than executions, but their lawyers had not been as clever as the coldly ambitious prosecutors. And so Darrow was dedicated to the proposition that no murderer he represented would be executed. And he never swerved from his course. He went to the bar for more than one hundred murderers in his time, and not a single one of them ever hit the hemp. More than that, at least a third of them got off scot free.

The Darrow who was so well known around the Criminal Courts Building—the scowling, shuffling, unkempt, magnetic Darrow who kept prosecutors awake nights—was exemplified in one murder case he handled—that of a Milquetoasty little man who chopped up his fat wife so that he could give his undivided attention to another woman. Here, if ever there was one, was a client whose ultimate end should be the gallows. But the little man had a well-filled sock, and Darrow, after examining its contents, decided to take the case.

So far as the evidence went, Darrow knew he didn't have a prayer. The prosecutor had the little man dead to rights. So there was no way of finding a loophole through the evidence. But there was always the jury—good men and true, perhaps, but not necessarily very bright. Darrow's only chance was somehow to put the defendant on an even, sympathetic basis with some of the jurors.

So Darrow saw to it when the jury was being picked that he got as wide a variety of men as possible—carpenters, store-keepers, old men, young men, single men, married men, fellows who liked baseball, soccer, basketball, fishing, and hunting.

The murderer had once kept a small store, he had liked to go to soccer matches, and he had liked to fish. Since Darrow had seen to it that two of the jurors kept small stores and half of them were soccer fans and that several liked to fish, the case was all set up for Darrow before the prosecutor even started to introduce the evidence. Darrow couldn't, of course, expect an acquittal. What he was after was a disagreement. If he could get one disagreement, he could get another, and another, and the case would be kicked around until it got lost.

After the prosecution evidence was in, Darrow didn't put his client on the stand. Instead, he carefully rehearsed the little murderer to sit meekly at the defense table, a picture of docility, while he summed up. Darrow addressed his remarks to the small storekeepers, the soccer fans, and the fishermen, and to hell with the others. He pictured his little client as having acted in self-defense against an overpowering woman.

"And then he cut her up," Darrow said, "out of sheer fright. Why, gentlemen, take a look at this poor little man. Does he look to you to be the kind of a man who would have so much as an evil thought? Just look at his pinched face and undernourished little body. Why, this brute of a woman that he was forced to kill to save his own life—why, gentlemen, she wouldn't even *feed* him. I tell you, gentlemen, I am defending this little man for nothing—he has no money, but that does not matter to me in this instance—I am defending him so that he can go back to his little business and eke out enough to keep body and soul together—and perhaps go to a soccer game once in a while and maybe do a little fishing, too."

It is easy to imagine what went on in the jury room. "The little sonofabitch ought to swing," we can hear a nonsporting carpenter saying to a small storekeeper who liked to fish.

"He should like hell," we can hear the storekeeper answering. "He would never do a thing like that unless he was driven into it. Why, he likes soccer and fishing. *I* like soccer and fishing. You goin' to stand there and tell me that I could cut up *my* wife?"

So of course Darrow got his disagreement. It was the same essential story at the little cut-up's second trial—and the same disagreement. Then Darrow, following the same line, got still a third disagreement. By that time the boys in the prosecutor's office were beginning to see how somebody *could* get mad enough to commit murder. They accepted a manslaughter plea, and, if Darrow had taken the time to carry the case further, would probably have settled for a breach of the peace.

There was once quite a stink in Chicago about some dental students cheating in their examinations by somehow getting hold of the answers in advance. A detective for a go-getting prosecutor learned that the son of an examiner had gotten hold of the answers from papa's briefcase and, realizing that he had practically struck gold, had gone out and sold the answers to the boys about to take the exams.

One of the purchasers had been foolish enough to pay the examiner's son by check, so when the gumshoe from the prosecutor's office laid hands on the canceled check, the jig was up. The answer seller, indicted for his illegal hustling, yelled for

Darrow, who grabbed the case because the defendant's old man could afford to pay a handsome fee to get his son off the hook.

The prosecutor put the guilty purchaser on the stand. "You admit," he said, "that you paid the defendant here the sum of money represented by this check so that he would supply you with the answers?" The witness, who looked as if he wished he had bitten his tongue off for admitting *any*thing, answered, "Yes."

While the witness was admitting this and that—all of it driving the defendant closer to a conviction—Darrow noticed that the fellow had an apparently painful right arm. And so, when it came time to cross-examine him, Darrow asked how he had hurt his arm.

"In jail," said the witness.

"In jail?" repeated Darrow. "You mean when you were taken to jail after they arrested you in this case?"

"Yes," answered the witness.

Darrow detected what he felt was an eagerness on the part of the witness to talk about what had happened to him in jail. He shot a side glance at the prosecutor and the prosecutor was looking the other way.

"Were you *beaten* in jail?" asked Darrow.

"Yes, I was," said the witness.

"Who beat you?" Somebody from the prosecutor's office had.

"Why?" asked Darrow.

"To make me confess that I paid for the examination answers."

"That," said Darrow, "will be all. *Quite* all."

Now Darrow turned to the jury. He didn't say a word. He just raised his eyebrows. That's all he had to do.

Darrow picked up his hat and coat when the jurors filed out to deliberate on their verdict. "Where are you going?" asked the defendant's father. "Aren't you going to stay to hear the verdict?"

"Why should I?" asked Darrow. "They can't do anything but bring in an acquittal." And of course he was right.

One day a woman—a widow supporting her three children —called at Darrow's office and asked if he would defend her. She had just been indicted for perjury. She didn't have any money to spend, but that did not always matter to Darrow. He had a genuine sympathy for little people in trouble and he was almost savage in his efforts to win acquittals for first offenders —and this woman would be a first offender.

The widow had a job as secretary to an insurance adjuster— her sole means of supporting herself and her children. It seemed that the insurance adjuster had been playing ball with an arson ring and had been accused of complicity in a plot whereby the ring had collected important money on a big fire. When brought to trial for his part in the conspiracy, the adjuster's only possible out was to prove that he had been away from Chicago the day of the fire. He hadn't been, of course, so he asked his secretary—the widow who had now come to Darrow to defend her—to lie for him by saying that he had been out of Chicago on business the day of the fire and that she had accompanied him. And so she testified to the lie when the adjuster was brought to trial, believing her employer to be innocent and willing to lie to save him—and to save her job.

The woman's testimony resulted in an acquittal for the adjuster. But the prosecutor, boiling mad at the adjuster's getting off through what he suspected was perjured testimony, put a dick on the case and learned that the woman had been in Chicago the day of the fire and had, therefore, lied on the stand

when her employer was tried. Thus she was indicted for perjury.

Darrow's sympathy was aroused by the woman's story. He
agreed to take the case for nothing. A couple of weeks later he
went to Springfield, to the office of Governor Frank Lowden,
an old friend. "Frank," he said, "I need a pardon for a client of
mine—a widow with three children to support. She is in trouble
simply because she tried to help her employer and save her job."

Then Darrow unfolded the whole story. Governor Lowden
was touched. He telephoned to the chairman of the parole
board and explained the situation. "Clarence," he said when he
hung up, "the chairman of the parole board wants to see you."

Now Darrow explained the whole thing—well, *practically*
the whole thing—to the chairman of the parole board. The
chairman listened sympathetically. "I agree with you, Mr. Darrow," he said. "No good purpose has been served by the conviction of this woman. She is an innocent victim of circumstances."
The chairman was jotting notes on a pad. "Now, Mr. Darrow,
just what was the date of this woman's conviction?"

"Oh," said Darrow, "she hasn't been convicted yet. Her trial
doesn't come up until next week."

The chairman blinked. This was a new one on him. It is still,
in fact, probably the only instance known in which a lawyer
has made an application for parole before his client has even
gone to trial. But Darrow was assured by the chairman that the
predicament of his client would be given prompt and sympathetic consideration once she was convicted.

Darrow saw to it that the story reached the papers. Some of
the jurors at the widow's trial read of Darrow's visit to the
governor. Since Darrow was fighting so hard for this woman,
she must be *innocent*. Anyway, what would be the use of con-
victing her if the pardon board was all set to throw a convic-

tion out the official window? That, in substance, was obviously how the jury felt. They acquitted the woman on the first ballot.

Such, then, was one side of Clarence Seward Darrow—the courtroom wizard and legal magician. But behind his razzle-dazzle surface—the surface, practically, of a shyster—was a great humanitarian. Some people said he had a split personality, that he led a double life. He alone knew the truth. When he wasn't producing nightmares for prosecuting attorneys, he was grinding away at good causes—important causes, too. He was for the little man all the way, he was for religious freedom though he had no religion of his own, and he despised, with all his heart, intolerance. Some of the things he accomplished didn't hit the front pages as his murder cases did, but they were far more important, affecting the life of every man, woman, and child in the United States today.

The first case that brought Darrow to national attention had its genesis the night of December 30, 1905, when Frank Steunenberg, ex-governor of Idaho, opened the front gate of his home in Caldwell and thus pulled a wire that set off an infernal machine that killed him. Steunenberg, who had started as a printer and become a small-time newspaper publisher, had been a great champion of the workingman. He had, in fact, been elected to the governorship largely through the support of the Western Federation of Miners—a rootin', tootin' hell-raising crew.

But the cordial relationship between Steunenberg and the miners' union had deteriorated during Steunenberg's gubernatorial regime. The Federation had called a strike in the mines in the Coeur d'Alene district and the governor had declared martial law to protect the mines—a move that the Federation regarded as a breach of faith on the part of the man they had helped put in office.

Pinkerton's National Detective Agency, hired by the mine owners to find the murderer, got a free-lance killer by the name of Harry Orchard in their sights and nabbed him. He told how he had made the bomb, shadowed Steunenberg, and planted the infernal device at an hour when he knew for sure that the prospective victim would be the next person to open the gate to his home.

It was what Orchard added to the Steunenberg part of his confession that brought Darrow into the case. Orchard said that he had been hired to murder the ex-governor by two officials of the Western Federation of Miners—Charles H. Moyer, the president, and William D. Haywood, the general secretary—and by a man named George Pettibone, an all-around champion of the workingman.

Moyer, Haywood, and Pettibone were quickly arrested and charged with the murder. The Western Federation of Miners summoned Darrow to defend the three accused men. Darrow quickly reduced the problem to its fundamentals. The state of Idaho would rely on the word of one man—Harry Orchard— to convict for murder three men who, whatever else they might have been, just weren't the murdering type.

While each side was preparing for the battle in the courtroom, Orchard was wined and dined and his biological urge catered to, all at the state's expense. The state knew how valuable he was to its case, and so did Orchard, so that everybody understood one another. Meantime, Darrow looked into Orchard's past. The man had committed more than a hundred murders for hire.

Testifying for the prosecution, Orchard was like an actor playing his first big part. He hammed it for a couple of days— dwelling on the details of his crime with the passion and gestures of a Shakespearean actor doing Hamlet's soliloquy. Darrow sat there studying the man and making notes.

When Darrow got hold of Orchard for cross-examination he tripped him up on dates, geography, and contradictions in his own testimony. Then Darrow dwelled on the fact that Orchard had committed more than a hundred murders. Everybody in the courtroom—including the jurors—was revolted. When it came time to address the jury, Darrow simply asked the good men and true if they felt like being responsible for jeopardizing the lives of three men on the testimony of the most heinous killer in criminal annals.

And then Darrow got down to real business—the business of ignoring the evidence and stabbing deep into the emotions of the twelve men who sat there listening to him. He made one of the great summations of his life that night in Idaho. The conviction of the defendants, he told the jury, would be a mortal blow to the cause of the workingman. "I speak," said Darrow, his voice taking on warmth, "for the poor, for the weak, for the weary, for that long line of men who, in darkness and despair, have borne the labors of the human race. Their eyes are upon you—upon you twelve men of Idaho—tonight." Darrow paused, lifted his head, and looked through a window of the courtroom into the blackness.

He began to speak now just loud enough for the jurors to hear him, and his voice was hoarse. "Out on our broad prairies, where men toil with their hands, out on the wide ocean where men are tossed and buffeted on the waves, through our mills and factories, and down deep under the earth, thousands of men and women and children—men who labor, men who suffer, women weary with care and toil—these men and these women and these children will kneel tonight and ask their God to guide your hearts." And now Darrow looked down from the sky and at the jurors again. He paused just long enough to search the face of each man. Then he said, "Yes, gentlemen, their eyes are upon you tonight."

Acquittal.

The general public pictured Darrow, because of his attire, as resembling a fugitive from Skid Row, a sort of grown-up ragamuffin. Actually, because of his wife—his second wife—he wore better-than-average clothes. It was what he did to his clothes during the course of a day that made him look unkempt —that and the fact that he looked upon a barber's chair with approximately the same degree of enthusiasm as a murderer looked upon the electric chair.

Darrow was never at ease if his black bow tie was correctly in place; he seldom got through a day without stuffing his coat pockets with miscellany having to do with the legal problem that was occupying him at the moment. If, in a cheap restaurant or lunchroom for a quick bite between morning and afternoon court sessions, some gravy from a hot roast-beef sandwich found its way from the plate to his vest, it stayed there.

Once Darrow was trying a case in which the opposing counsel was J. Hamilton Lewis, he of the pink whiskers, who later went to the United States Senate. Lewis was a regular fop when it came to clothes and was known as the Chesterfield of the Middle West—lavender suits, with cravats and spats to match— because he was as smooth in deportment as in dress.

During the case in which he opposed Darrow, Lewis would appear in court each morning, fresh out of a bandbox—cane, yellow gloves, and all, his pink whiskers glistening in the shafts of early sunlight. When the judge appeared, Lewis would make a production of the event. He would bow from the waist, pay his respects to His Honor, do likewise to the jury, and then favor Darrow with similar Chesterfieldian courtesy.

Darrow would look with jaundiced eye on the Lewis performances. Something had to happen. One morning Darrow, not having got home until very late the night before, arrived, spectacularly unkempt, half an hour late for the opening of court. The judge sitting impatiently on the bench, raised his eyebrows by way of inquiring for an explanation. Darrow, who usually reserved for most judges an attitude just short of open contempt, astonished everyone by making a Lewisian production of his apology to His Honor, and to the jury. Then, turning to the stiffly outraged Lewis, he outstretched his arms. "And as for *you*, sweetheart," he growled, "*kiss* me."

Darrow held a strong fascination for women as well as for men. "The damned fools," he once told a friend, "either want to press my pants or go to bed with me." The man was right. Between marriages, he met a sob sister on a Chicago newspaper who did both.

Clarence Seward Darrow was born on April 18, 1857, in the village of Kinsman in the rolling farmlands of Ohio, the fifth of eight children. He was to say in later life that it was obvious that he personally had nothing to do with getting born and that had he known about life in advance and been given a choice in the matter he would most likely have declined the adventure.

Clarence's father, Amirus Darrow, a brilliant and scholarly man, had studied for the Methodist ministry, but had given it up for carpentry. The end of all wisdom, he had concluded, was the fear of God, and the beginning of doubt was the beginning of wisdom. Thus Clarence became an agnostic.

So far as he was ever able to recall, Clarence Darrow was fourteen when he decided to become a lawyer. The village tinsmith, who was also the village justice of the peace, lived right across the street from the Darrows. His Honor dispensed justice, if it could be called that, after he had climbed down from the roofs for the day. Clarence, sitting on his front porch of a soft summer evening, would hear the sounds of squabbles from His Honor's chambers. When, finally, he decided to investigate, he was fascinated.

More often than not, the litigants acted as their own counsel, for the legal problems for the most part consisted of such matters as who was responsible for a broken window or who, during a heated discussion, had splattered tobacco juice in the other man's face first. Once in a while, though, in a more serious fight, a genuine lawyer would come from a nearby town. The visiting mouthpiece was usually something of a dandy, occasionally even wearing striped pants, and young Darrow decided then and there that if *he* were to have anything to do with deciding the merits of the litigation he would lean *away* from the fellow in the striped pants.

Darrow observed something else at these more serious litigations before the justice of the peace. Right did not always win; justice did not always triumph. On more than one occasion, Darrow saw the litigant he thought to be in the right have the case go against him because the other litigant had imported a dressy, fast-talking, fast-thinking mouthpiece. Clarence was never to forget that.

The big time in Kinsman was Fourth of July. Clarence's father and another carpenter would construct a wooden stand in the village square and come the Fourth it would be populated by out-of-town windbags talking about patriotism. Although only a kid, Clarence could tell that the orators for the most part had about as much sincerity as an auctioneer, yet the peasants who stood in the hot sun around the stand were deeply impressed. What young Darrow observed at these patriotic celebrations helped, too, to shape his destiny. It became an article of faith with him that people were, for the most part, stupid, and would believe practically anything if it were dished up in an appetizing form—and he was to prove it in courtrooms over and over again.

Darrow's regular education ended after he had finished the equivalent of one year of high school. The panic of 1873, which struck when he was sixteen, made it imperative that he go to work. He taught rural school for three years, but, sticking to his ambition to be a lawyer, studied law books not only at night but during school hours while the class dolt was shifting from one foot to another trying to recall who it was who discovered America.

By the time he had put away enough money from his schoolteaching to go to law school, Darrow was nineteen. He was a medium-sized fellow, loose-jointed, big-boned, and quizzical of eye. His face was broad, his brow was high, and usually it was partially obscured by a shock of hair that kept coming down in front. He had spent a good deal of time in the midwestern sun during summer vacations from schoolteaching, playing baseball, his favorite daytime pastime, and his face was already deeply lined. When, on his eightieth birthday, he was interviewed by a reporter for *The New York Times* he asked the reporter, "Do I look old?" The reporter answered, "Mr. Darrow, you have *always* looked old."

The young Darrow spoke slowly with a midwestern drawl. His voice wasn't so unusual as what was behind it. It was rich with sincerity, whether he was expressing a political opinion around the village cracker barrel or, while engaged in a favorite after-dark occupation, announcing that he would put the green ball in the side pocket. He smoked cigarets and once in awhile a cigar, and he took a drink with the boys, but liquor was never to be a weakness. He had, at the age of twenty, always been so occupied with one thing or another, that he had never had time to look twice at a girl. Darrow spent two years studying law—one year at a law school in Ann Arbor, Michigan, and another year in a law office in Youngstown, Ohio. Then, at the age of twenty-one, he tacked up a shingle in a little place called Andover, only ten miles from his birthplace.

Young Darrow never got off the ground in Andover. In two years of practice there his talents were confined to legal litigations in which the dairy farmers of the community became involved. The farmers took their milk to the butter and cheese factories of the region. Somewhere between the cows and the factories, the milk acquired a high water content. Church membership by the farmer culprits had no effect whatsoever on these cases of dilution since it was so easy to pour a bucketful of water into a milk can that many otherwise upright men could not resist. Darrow usually got the milk waterers off because in those days there was no scientific way of establishing the degree of richness of the cow juice and Darrow was just the boy to make the most of that.

So, when he was twenty-three, Darrow moved to the town of Ashtabula, some twenty-five miles further on. There he was elected city solicitor at a salary of $75 a month, with the right to take his own cases on the side. One case that he handled in Ashtabula cast shadows of coming events, revealing, as it did, Darrow's sympathy for the underdog, his disregard for money, and his tenacity of purpose.

A teen-age boy had attended a wealthy farmer during the farmer's illness and, as payment, had been given a horse harness worth $15. The farmer, upon recovering his health, decided, for some reason, he wanted the harness back. The boy refused to return it. He was brought to trial before a justice of the peace. He got Darrow to defend him, putting up Darrow's fee of $5.

The jury disagreed and the case had to be tried a second time. The boy had run out of money by now and Darrow said he would defend him for nothing. At the second trial the case was decided against the boy and the justice of the peace ordered him to return the harness to the man. "Don't do it," Darrow instructed his client. "We'll take the case to the Court of Common Pleas." There Darrow, still working for free, won the case.

Now the farmer carried the litigation to the Court of Appeals. There the verdict of the lower court was reversed and Darrow and the boy were back where they had started—all on the original $5. Much time had passed by now and Darrow had established himself in Chicago. There he carried the case to the State Supreme Court and, eight years after the Indian giver had first instituted legal action, the reversal of the Court of Appeals was reversed and the verdict in Darrow's client's favor was allowed to stand.

It was while practicing in Ashtabula that Darrow, who by this time had an eye for the girls and who had come to know his way around a hay ride, fell in love. He married a highly moral young lady named Ohl—Jessie Ohl—whose family had been friendly with his family. In a year or so they had a son, Paul—Darrow's only child.

The little family lived in a rented house and the years began to roll on. When he was about thirty, and had become the most prominent man in Ashtabula, Darrow decided to buy a house. As a result of that decision, his whole life was changed. Had it not been for this, Darrow might have lived out his days as a country lawyer, growing up with a country town, and then at the end being buried in a little hillside cemetery.

Darrow was about to close a deal for a house when the wife of the seller backed out. Darrow suddenly decided to move to

Chicago. He lived there in a cheap flat on the South Side and rented desk space in a downtown firetrap.

During his first decade in Chicago, the going was tough. There were more lawyers in the town than there was business for them and Darrow accomplished nothing to raise himself above the level of ambulance chaser. He grabbed any sort of case that came along—collecting bad bills for merchants, representing little people in accident cases, and so on.

One of Darrow's first clients in the early years was a snappy trigger-brained fellow named Joe Weil, later to be known to every police department in the English-speaking world as the Yellow Kid, confidence man *de luxe*. Weil had just given somebody a fast shuffle and the mark squawked. Darrow, deceived into thinking that he might be able to steer an intelligent fellow like Weil straight for the future, went into court with the Yellow Kid and convinced the jury that his poor misguided client, brimming over with the zest of youth, had merely perpetrated a prank—a serious prank, to be sure—but just a prank none the less.

The jury acquitted Weil. "All right, Joe," said Darrow, "now your whole life lies ahead of you. Never let me see you in trouble again." In later years when Weil, now notorious for his confidence work, ran afoul of the wrong kind of mark and faced another jolt in durance vile, he called on Darrow to defend him. Darrow turned down the Kid. He didn't like Weil. "Anyway," Darrow later said, "you can't cure con men. It's in their blood."

Even in his earlier years Darrow seemed to have a sixth sense that defined for him in advance just how much he could get out of a jury. Often he played it all the way, for an acquittal; sometimes he knew he would be getting the best for his client if he voided the death penalty and got a prison term.

One man, freshly jailed for murder, hollered for Darrow. The man had just murdered his landlord for raising his rent—an act that aroused considerably less sympathy then than it would today. Darrow went to see the prisoner. The man's appearance was against him; he would have made a splendid exhibit many years later when Darrow, spearheading the defense in the Scopes "monkey trial," embraced the theory that man and the apes were descended from a common ancestral species. The prisoner offered Darrow a large fee—but there was a catch to it. Darrow had to get him off; cheating the gallows wouldn't be enough. Darrow said he thought the very best he could get would be a prison term. No soap. The ape man got another mouthpiece—and the gallows.

A couple of elderly peddlers, smart characters, went into the business of buying used barrels from one department of a big meat-packing plant and selling the same barrels back to another department of the same plant at more than double the price— a practice which, from the viewpoint of certain gentlemen in business with the United States government later, was years ahead of its time. The dodge was so successful that the peddlers, smelling bigger money, began to mix phantom barrels in with the real barrels. A checker for the packing company took up residence among the barrels and over a period of weeks jotted down in a large notebook columns of figures—all designed to disclose that the packing company was being swindled. So the packing company yelled for the law, the peddlers were placed on trial, and there was Darrow to defend them—knowing they were dripping with guilt but wondering how to clothe them in innocence.

The figures jotted down by the man who had resided in the barrels constituted the state's principal evidence against the culprits. The book containing the figures was offered in evidence. Darrow, examining the book, saw that the figures, though meaningful to the man who had made them, and also meaningful to the state, were just a meaningless jumble to him. He knew, though, that he dared not question the man who had put down the figures; the eavesdropper from the barrel colony would no doubt be able to make them clear to the jurors if put through a cross-examination. So Darrow allowed the book to pass into evidence without objection so that the jurors, seeing it for the first time, would be as confused by it as he was.

Right after Darrow waived objection to the book, the judge declared a noon recess. Darrow was not going to put the defendants on the stand; he couldn't afford to. So after the noon recess each side would sum up, the judge would charge the jury, and the twelve citizens would retire to deliberate on the verdict.

A friend of Darrow's happened to be in the same elevator with the jurors when they were going down for lunch. He overheard one of them asking another why Darrow hadn't objected to the introduction of the book. "Must be something fishy about that book," answered the second juror. "Maybe Darrow is going to spring a surprise when he sums up."

When his friend tipped him to the overheard conversation, Darrow knew the verdict was as good as in the bag.

"Gentlemen," he said to the jurors, "maybe you are smarter than I am and can make something out of the figures in that book. But I'll be darned if I can. All I know is that those figures can be twisted around to make a point of practically anything."

All Darrow asked was that the jurors study the figures carefully, see if they could make any sense whatsoever out of them, then search their hearts and determine whether, on the basis of the figures, they were justified in sending the two defendants —"these poor, ragged men, trying to keep body and soul together in the short time remaining to them on this troubled planet"—to prison. And of course the jurors decided to acquit the defendants—thus clearing the way for the two poor, ragged old men to devote themselves, in the short time remaining to them on this troubled planet, to better and bigger swindles.

As Darrow became more widely known, and occasionally collected a big fee for a civil action or through a criminal action in which he resorted to courtroom stratagems such as that which got the two old barrel dealers off, his home life began to come apart at the seams. His wife, Jessie, had failed to keep pace with him. They were divorced.

Darrow took up with a mistress—a physically and mentally stimulating woman with auburn hair. They played house for a while and then she began to have visions of making it legal. But she had picked the wrong man. Darrow by this time had become an apostle of free love. Marriage, he believed, was for morons.

Darrow became, in the courtrooms, an authentically unkempt figure, as would any man who slept in his clothes. "Counsel," a judge said to him one morning, "looks very tired." Said Darrow, "Your Honor would be tired, too, if he went through what I went through last night." But Darrow's unkempt appearance was at least partly window dressing. He had noticed that jurors frequently felt antagonized by a mouthpiece far above them on the sartorial level. The average juror had shiny pants that were pressed twice a year; Darrow's slovenly attire put him in the juror's class.

Darrow was trying one case where he didn't have a prayer. His client, a stockyard worker, had chopped his wife's head off. As the case wore on, Darrow could have chopped his own head off for taking it. He had made a mistake about the defendant. He had felt sorry for the man when he had asked to be defended; now he realized his client was a fiend incarnate. But there he was, stuck with it, and with a reputation to defend—a reputation that was already marking him as a lawyer who had never had a client executed. What to do?

It happened that the lawyer for the state prided himself on his attire; not only that, he positively looked down on men who were careless in dress. So that night Darrow rubbed the elbows of his jacket with sandpaper until they were threadbare and carefully scuffed up his shoes. Next morning his appearance was too much for the prosecutor. He said nothing, but the way he looked Darrow up and down was practically audible. Darrow, playing his role with Shakespearean emphasis, hung his head a little, but, sneaking an eye-corner view of the jurors, saw that they, brothers under the unkempt attire, were sorry for him. It was all over but the verdict. The jury acquitted the beheader.

By the time he was in his early forties, Darrow had arrived at the decision that picking a jury was the most important part of any case. "Get the right men in the box," he said, "and the rest is window dressing." Darrow seldom accepted a German or a Swede for a jury. A German, he held, was too bullheaded, and a Swede too stubborn. Some historians credit Darrow with originating, in a sour moment, the joke that the only thing dumber than a dumb Irishman was a smart Swede. Irishmen and Jews, when Darrow could get them, were his favorite jurors; both, he held, were highly emotional and easily moved to sympathy. The perfect jury, to his way of thinking, was one comprising six Irishmen and six Jews. "Give me that combination in the box," he once said, "and I could get Judas Iscariot off with a five-dollar fine." As a general rule, Darrow preferred older jurors to younger ones. An older man had seen more of life, he thought, than a younger one. Thus an older man would be more sympathetic with the jams other men got into and have a better understanding of the motivating forces that had culminated in the trouble.

When an important case was coming up, Darrow assigned investigators to look into the lives of prospective jurors. Sometimes this was an extensive and prolonged procedure, depending on the importance of the impending case. Thus, before he even went into the courtroom on a really big case he had what amounted to a dossier on all the veniremen—their likes and dislikes, their prejudices, their foibles, what lodges they belonged to, and so on.

But Darrow went even further than that. When questioning a prospective juror who was, because of advance information, completely acceptable to him, Darrow would ask the man questions that had no bearing whatever on his acceptable characteristics, thus throwing the prosecution off the track.

Occasionally, Darrow would handle a civil case, especially if it was against a big public-utilities company. He hated big corporations and was always willing to take a crack at them, even at his own expense, just for the hell of it.

He became nevertheless, the great apostle of compromise in big damage suits. He always looked at three sides of every litigation—the litigant's side, the defendant's side, and his own side. Intuitively he knew when compromise was the better part of valor. He saw little use in getting into a fight when staying out of it would prove more profitable. Better to get five thousand dollars by writing a few letters to the lawyers on the other side than to spend weeks preparing a case. But if the big companies insisted on going into the ring, Darrow would go in there swinging.

One time a man walked into Darrow's office and asked him to take a case against a public-utilities company. The man had been injured by falling debris. Darrow, in the offhand way he had, scribbled some notes about the case on a piece of paper and stuffed the paper in his pocket. Some weeks later the public-utilities company sent Darrow a letter saying they were willing to settle with Mr. So-and-So for such-and-such a sum.

Darrow was mystified. "What the hell's this about?" he asked his secretary. The secretary said she was sure she didn't know. Then Darrow recalled the man who had been in his office some weeks previously. "Good Christ!" he said, "I never got around to doing anything about that case. I wonder what has happened?"

What had happened was that the litigant had telephoned the public-utilities company right after seeing Darrow, informing it that Darrow was on the case. The company's lawyers, construing Darrow's silence to mean that he was up to something that would just about ruin them, had decided to get the case cleaned up as quickly as possible and had thus voluntarily offered him a settlement. Darrow took it, keeping only a small percentage of the take for himself.

There is no record of how much money Darrow averaged in a year. Unquestionably, he had a few $100,000 years in the days when a dollar wasn't a dime with the tax taken out. Yet he never had any money. In fact, he was usually in debt. He contributed large sums to various causes he was interested in and never said anything about it. He was always good for a handout to unfortunates who shuffled into his office. Sometimes in saving some cornered moron from the noose he laid out large sums of his own in investigations pertinent to the case with never a prayer for so much as a dollar for a fee. And to top it all off, Darrow was an unfortunate market speculator. He was a sucker for a fast-talking gold-brick salesman who caught him between trials. He once said that he had almost enough phony stock certificates to paper his apartment.

Darrow's offices and his places of abode were just as casual as the man was. He had one desk—a great big battered affair—that he took with him when he moved from office to office. The desk was usually piled high with papers and he could seldom find what he was looking for.

He lived in apartments most of his life. They were so sparsely furnished, and the carpeting so nearly threadbare, that one visiting New York lawyer, going into a Darrow apartment for the first time, thought for a moment that he had stumbled into the wrong place.

Darrow liked nothing better in an accident case than to cross-examine a doctor testifying for the other side—a doctor who would say that the accident victim who was suing, though confined to a wheel chair, would no doubt be up and around in good time. His favorite device in dealing with such a sawbones ran thusly:

"You came here from out of town to testify for the company, Doctor?"

"Yes, Mr. Darrow."

"And you had a nice trip?"

"Yes, Mr. Darrow."

"How much are you getting for testifying, Doctor—over and above the expenses of your trip?"

"Three hundred dollars, Mr. Darrow."

Darrow would thereupon turn to the jury, raise his eyebrows and, still looking at the jury rather than at the witness, growl, "That will be all, Doctor."

Darrow liked to joust not only with doctors for the other side but with *any* expert for the opposition. He had a strong affinity for puncturing balloons. Once he was representing a sea captain named Erickson—John Erickson—charged with criminal negligence in a maritime disaster. Erickson had been the captain of a Great Lakes steamer, the *Eastland*, which, while lying at a dock in Chicago, preparatory to embarking on a cruise with hundreds of holiday-makers, capsized with a frightful loss of life—one of the worst civilian disasters in American history. Although the ship had just been officially inspected and found seaworthy, the public hue and cry reached such a crescendo that somebody had to be made responsible. So Captain Erickson, a man with an unblemished maritime record, was nominated for occupancy of a prison cell.

The principal witness for the state was a university professor —a man hardly given to false modesty. In his cross-examination of the professor, Darrow, having boned up on ship construction, put the witness through a long series of questions having to do with the construction of a ship. The professor knew all the answers.

"What the hell are you doing, Clarence?" whispered an associate counsel. "You're building the man up."

"That's exactly what I want to do," answered Darrow, "the better to knock him down."

When the professor had been properly built up, Darrow asked him who, in his opinion, was the world's foremost authority on ship construction.

"Why," answered the professor, "*I* am."

"And who," inquired Darrow, "would you say was the *second* greatest authority on ship construction?" The professor named a naval architect in Scotland.

"And the third greatest authority?" The professor said there was no such animal; only he and the man in Scotland really knew all there was to know about ship construction.

"I see," said Darrow. "Then the defendant here—Captain

Erickson—would hardly be in the same class as you and that man in Scotland when it comes to knowing all there is to know about ship construction."

"That's right, sir."

"Then Captain Erickson couldn't possibly have known enough about ship construction to have known that, in spite of officially approved examinations of the *Eastland*, it would tip over when the weight of all those poor people was concentrated on one side of it."

"That's right, sir."

"Then Captain Erickson couldn't possibly have been responsible for the *Eastland* disaster?"

"That," said the expert, before he realized what was coming out of his mouth, "is right, sir." And that, of course, acquitted Captain John Erickson of the *Eastland* disaster.

When he needed expert medical opinion for his own side, Darrow firmly believed that he could find a doctor who would testify to practically anything. That is to say, a man could be the picture of health—a condition to which ninety-nine doctors would subscribe—yet the hundredth medical practitioner would take the view that the man was on the brink of eternity.

Darrow had occasion to look around for that hundredth doctor in the case of a client who had, while in a position of public trust, freely availed himself of the contents of the public till. The man was in such fine physical and mental shape that he could have passed the stiffest of insurance examinations, but, as Darrow saw the case, the only way to save the crook from prison was to convince a jury that he was a physical and mental wreck.

So Darrow hunted around until he found a doctor who wasn't doing so well in his practice. Would the doctor like to make a

nice fee for testifying to the poor condition of his client? *Would*
he!

At the trial, Darrow didn't let on to the prosecution what
his defense would be. In fact, he misled the prosecution into
thinking that he was going to attack their evidence—black-and-
white bank statements proving the defendant was a thief—
by yelling objections or making furious notes when the mone-
tary testimony went in.

Then Darrow put his doctor on the stand. "Would you say,"
Darrow asked the sawbones, "that the defendant here is in
fairly sound physical and mental health?" The doctor looked
shocked—shocked that such a thing could be so much as
thought of. The defendant was far from being in sound physical
and mental health. He was, in fact, a physical wreck and,
mentally, a candidate for the nut house. "You mean, Doctor,"
asked Darrow, "that the defendant hasn't long to live?"

"Hasn't long to *live?*" repeated the witness. "Why, I
wouldn't be a bit surprised if he never left this courtroom alive."
Now the doctor went into the horrible details. Darrow looked
at the defendant; the rascal although bubbling with health,
seemed to be wracked by pain and riddled with disease. Now
Darrow looked at the jury. He raised his eyebrows but he didn't
speak. He didn't have to. The jurors, having heard the dire tid-
ings, were filled with consuming sympathy for the defendant.
And of course they acquitted the man.

Darrow was defending another crook one time—a cripple—
and, though the fee was good, he didn't have much of a case.
He didn't, in fact, have *any* case. Here again was a man about
to draw a one-way ticket to the big house. But Darrow kept
pondering the fact that the man was a cripple and wondering
how he could put such a misfortune on a favorable basis.
Finally he got an idea. He sent an investigator to look into the

backgrounds of the panel of good men and true from which the jury would be drawn. He wanted to find out who among the prospective jurors had any cripples in their families. His investigator quickly found that one juror had a crippled brother. That juror was quickly accepted by Darrow.

The state's case against the crippled defendant was one of those open-and-shut affairs. Once again Darrow had to throw the legal aspects of the problem into the discard and put it on an emotional basis. In his summation, he shaped his remarks almost entirely for the benefit of the juror who had the crippled brother. Would these good men and true find it in their hearts to send this poor, deformed man to prison—no matter what he had done? And so on and so on and so on. By the time Darrow was through, not only the juror with the crippled brother was touched, but most of the men in the box were in tears. The crippled crook was quickly acquitted.

Another time Darrow was defending a man who had skipped out on a loan shark. This one would be easy. Well he knew that most people have, at one time or another, felt the screws being put to them for nonpayment of a loan. Again he sent an investigator out to find out which members of the jury panel had been hounded by a friendly loan outfit. At least half of them had. So, when the case went to trial, the prosecution was trying a dead beat and Darrow was trying the loan shark. Darrow of course won.

As his reputation spread, Darrow, although best known for his courtroom legerdemain, engaged in greatly diversified work. Bernarr Macfadden, the great physical culturist, was constantly holding cracked-wheat derbies in which non-meat eaters, wearing only loin cloths and running shoes, periodically panted through twenty-five miles of countryside, to show the marvelous dietary benefits of cracked wheat. Occasionally, during these exhibitions, some narrow-minded rural cops would pull in a physical culturist for indecent exposure and Macfadden would yell for Darrow. Darrow would usually get the trouble settled somehow or other, using every trick short of the dodge that a naked runner, purple with cold, had not really been naked at all but had been wearing a tight-fitting blue-serge suit.

One night, while Darrow was giving a lecture in Chicago, he kept looking at a pretty red-haired girl down front. He had by now been playing the field for some time, and playing it well, all the while preaching the benefits of free love. But this night, as he looked at the red-haired girl in the audience (she seemed to be in her middle twenties, some twenty years younger than he) something happened to him. He fell in love.

The girl was sitting with friends of Darrow's—the John H. Greggs, Gregg being the originator of the Gregg system of shorthand. Darrow telescoped his speech, got down off the platform, and shoved his way through his admirers to the Greggs.

"John," he said, "give me an introduction to the young lady."

Gregg, who knew Darrow quite well, drew him to one side. "It won't do you any good, Clarence," he said. "She's engaged."

"To hell with that," said Darrow. "I'm going to marry that girl. Introduce me."

Gregg introduced Darrow to Ruby Hamerstrom—a brilliant, soundly educated and socially conscious young lady. "Let's go out somewhere," Darrow said to Miss Hamerstrom. "I've fallen in love with you."

Ruby Hamerstrom laughed. "You must be crazy, Mr. Darrow," she said.

"Maybe I am," said Darrow, "but that doesn't alter the fact that I'm in love with you. Let's go out somewhere."

Ruby Hamerstrom was part Swedish and had a mind of her own. She didn't go out with Darrow. Next day he began to phone her and send her telegrams and flowers. She fought a delaying action for weeks. One night she told her fiance about Darrow. "Well," said the fiance, "why don't you see him, explain once and for all that we're about to be married, and he'll stop annoying you."

That proved to be the worst advice any fiance has ever given any fiancee. Ruby Hamerstrom saw Darrow and, overcome by the man's combination of charms, fell in love with him and married him. She remained with him to the end—the great love affair of Darrow's life.

The curtain ascended on a perilous period in the career of Clarence Darrow when, about one o'clock of a morning in the spring of 1910, somebody set off a dynamite blast in the building of the *Los Angeles Times*. In the resultant explosion and fire, twenty-one *Times* employes were killed. William J. Burns, one of the cleverest detectives this country has ever produced, was assigned to track down the killers. Darrow loved Burns as Cain loved Abel and *vice versa*. Burns got on the right trail immediately. The crime, he knew, was the result of labor strife. Various unions were trying to make Los Angeles a closed-shop city, and the *Times* was the mouthpiece of the open-shop opposition. The *Times* was published by an old fire-eater—General Harrison Gray Otis, a Civil War hero with a fierce countenance and handsome goatee—who baited the unionists. The general had small cannon mounted in strategic spots throughout the *Times* plant. "Let the bastards start something," he used to growl as he prowled the premises, "and, by God, I'll finish it!"

Burns soon smelled out the masterminds of the plot—two really bad boys named McNamara—brothers J. J. and J. B. Then he located another cog in the murder machine—a fellow named Ortie McManigal. McManigal confessed every detail of the plot, implicating the McNamara brothers and others, and the McNamaras were arrested and charged with the twenty-one deaths.

Samuel Gompers, the head of the American Federation of Labor, asked Darrow to defend the McNamaras. The fee was big and Darrow was short of money.

The first thing Darrow did was to try to establish the fiction that all the McNamara brothers had meant to do, when planting the dynamite, was to *scare* the nonunion workers in the *Times* plant. It wasn't the dynamite that caused all the havoc, but a gas explosion and fire that followed the comparatively harmless blast.

He hired architects and engineers to make a small reproduction of the *Times* building, inside and out, and proposed to go into court and prove to the jury that the dynamite itself could not possibly have caused the deaths.

But William J. Burns, playing the other side of the street, was too smart for Darrow this time. He dug up evidence showing that the dynamite that the McNamaras had ordered from a powder-manufacturing company in the San Francisco Bay area had been made especially powerful at their specifications.

Darrow hired a private eye—a fellow named Bert Franklin— for the twin purposes of spying on Burns and what he was up to, and to get lines on the lives and habits of the prospective jurors who would sit in judgment on the McNamaras. Burns caught on to what Darrow was doing and put counterspies to work on Franklin. Darrow, learning of this, put counterspies on the counterspies, then Burns, ever apace, put counterspies on the counterspies who were counterspying on the original spies. It was some fun. The spying and counterspying reached such proportions that Darrow knew when Burns was in need of a laxative and Burns knew what Darrow would have for breakfast in the morning even before Darrow knew himself.

Then an odd thing happened. Nobody knows to this day how it came about. Although the prosecution had enough on the McNamara brothers to hang them and then electrocute their corpses, the prosecution decided to accept pleas of guilty from both brothers. Consequently, J. J., the elder brother, drew life, and the younger one got off with fifteen years. The country was amazed. Everybody, especially Burns, wondered how Darrow had pulled it.

Then somebody in the district attorney's office put Franklin, Darrow's head spy, in the sights. Franklin was arrested and shown some rubber hose. He said that Darrow had paid him to purchase two prospective jurors. Franklin had, in fact, paid four hundred dollars to one of them. So Darrow was indicted for conspiracy to corrupt two jurors. He would be tried twice —once for each allegedly purchased juror. This was pretty bad business. Darrow was now in the fifty-third year of his life— no longer a kid who could brush off a charge like that and live long enough for people to forget it.

Darrow, the great lawyer, now needed a lawyer to defend him. He chose the man who is remembered to this day as the most flamboyant mouthpiece in the history of American jurisprudence—Earl Rogers, a blindingly brilliant, strikingly handsome, and exceedingly corrupt attorney who was drunk half the time.

Rogers built up a pretty good case for his client Darrow. He would show that Franklin, Darrow's accuser, was a man whose word had long been regarded as worthless. The trouble was that the bottle got in the way of the defense that Rogers was constructing for Darrow. So Rogers made things brief, then turned the Darrow defense over to Darrow himself.

All during the trial, Darrow had been a beaten man. Now the old magic came back to him, and the inner fires suddenly burned white. He dramatized his whole life while the jury sat entranced. He had made many mistakes in his life, he told the jury, but crookedness had never been one of them. Was the jury, then willing to destroy him—and all the poor souls he hoped to save from injustice before he died—on the word of this scoundrel Franklin? Anyway, what good would be accomplished by sending him to prison? He was, he pointed out, already under sentence of death—even as every man who sat before him in the jury box was sentenced to death. The jurors seemed shocked. Darrow smiled sadly. Every man, he pointed out, in the words of Oliver Wendell Holmes, was sentenced to death for the crime of living.

The jury acquitted him. One down, one to go.

While Darrow was awaiting trial on the charge of conspiracy to corrupt the second juror, an old acquaintance appeared—a scowling, big-boned fellow named George Bissett. A few years before this, Bissett had been a client of Darrow's in Chicago. Darrow had gotten him off for killing a cop in a barroom pistol duel on the plea that the cop had fired first. Bissett had vowed then that he would never forget Darrow. And he hadn't. He had ridden the rods from the Midwest to do what he could for Darrow after reading how this character Franklin was saying those things about Darrow.

Darrow was touched. "What do you propose to do, George?" he asked Bissett.

"Kill the sonofabitch," said Bissett. "I brought some dynamite to blow up his house."

Darrow invoked all his eloquence to dissuade Bissett from his play. It was no dice. Bissett was a true friend. Nobody was going to get away with doing anything to the man who had got him off that murder rap.

Somebody (could it have been Darrow?) tipped the police

that George Bissett should be picked up as a vagrant. And so Bissett was pinched and shipped back to the Midwest where he was murdered for playing too fast and too loose with the wrong woman. Darrow caught his breath and went on trial for the second charge. Rogers was up to his old failings again. One day he was in court, the next he wasn't. This time the jury disagreed. Then the charge against Darrow was dropped.

As the years rolled by, Clarence Seward Darrow, now the best-known lawyer in Chicago, had more cases offered to him than he could possibly handle. He moved from office to office sometimes in partnership with others, sometimes by himself. But even when he was in partnership, a partner was usually reduced to the status of the fifth wheel on the wagon. If a case came into the office that required intensive research over dry statutes, Darrow would pass it on to a partner. But if something cropped up that had the makings of a big courtroom show Darrow would grab it.

Once an out-of-state evangelist walked into his office and asked if Darrow would defend him on a young lady's charge that he was the father of her unborn child.

"Well, *are* you?" asked Darrow.

"I don't know," said the evangelist. "I *could* be, but I would have to be sure." Darrow asked the preacher how he was fixed for paying the expenses of an investigation into the complainant's background, in addition to the Darrow fee. Money was no object; the evangelist was loaded. Darrow got the impression that the man of God had been short-circuiting some of the collection money, but that was no skin off his teeth.

A couple of Darrow investigators learned that the young lady who had succumbed to the evangelist had been quite a girl and that any one of a dozen or more young studs in the town where she lived could very well have been responsible for her condition. What the girl really had her eye on was part of that short-circuited collection money. So Darrow sent an emissary to the girl's father, pointing out that he would be forced to subpoena several of the local boys to testify to their relations with his daughter if the girl went through with her suit. So the matter was settled out of court for a few hundred dollars.

Not long afterward, the evangelist was spreading the word of God in a Chicago suburb and Darrow, being in the vicinity, attended a service. There was his ex-client, up in the pulpit exhorting the sinners to repent, warning that Judgment Day was in the offing. Next day, Darrow made a notable remark to one of his partners about evangelists. There lies buried in the heart of every evangelist, he said, the wreck of a confidence man.

Although Darrow had never patronized brothels—"Why," he once said, "should I *pay* for it?"—he had a strong affinity for madams and their girls. "After all," he used to say, "they're serving a good purpose and giving value for value received. What's so wrong about that?" And so he was always glad to defend a madam, or a girl, or a group of girls, feeling, in that big heart of his, that they were victims of circumstances.

Once, then, he was defending a madam and half a dozen of her little doves, who had been caught in a raid by a couple of hard-hearted cops. One particular cop was to be the principal witness, so Darrow looked into him. "Don't worry," he said to a lawyer he was sharing an office with at the time, "the case is as good as won."

When the cop—a righteous-looking man with a wife and family—was through testifying to what he had come upon in the den of iniquity, Darrow went to work on him, slowly, gently, deceptively. "You have testified here that the lady who runs this establishment offered you a bribe and that you spurned it. Is that right?" It was. "Of course you wouldn't do such a thing as accept a bribe from anybody."

"No, sir, I certainly would not."

"You have, then, been offered many bribes when raiding these houses of ill fame, as you choose to call them, but you have turned down every dollar that was ever offered to you. Is that right?" It was right.

"Now," Darrow went on, "let me ask you something else. While you have raided a good many of these places, you have not always been successful in gaining entrance and thus obtaining evidence. Is that so?" That was so.

"Do you happen to have a record of the establishments where you were unsuccessful in gaining entrance—and the dates when you tried to gain entrance?" No, the officer did not have such data.

"Well," said Darrow, "I have. Maybe I can refresh your memory." Darrow, through a pipeline right in the police department, began to reel off a list of joints that had been unsuccessfully approached by the witness and the dates of the official failures. The witness clearly recalled each dud raid and the date it had been made.

Now Darrow began to question the cop about how much pay he got, how much it cost him to live, how much, if anything, he saved, and what other income he had, if any, aside from his police pay. The cop practically broke into tears as he told Darrow how difficult it was for him to make ends meet on his police pay—his only source of income.

Darrow, who had, through devious methods of his own, established a pipeline in the bank where the witness had an account, reeled off the records of the cop's deposits. The prosecutor started to scream that the cop's bank account had nothing to do with the case. Darrow maintained that it did. The judge allowed him to proceed. What Darrow divulged, in reading the dates and deposit figures from the bank, was that the cop had made a sizable deposit after each unsuccessful raid. The inference was clear. In his summation, Darrow threw the issue at hand—the charge that the madam and the girls had been caught in carnal pursuits in violation of the law—right out the window. Before he was through, the jury thought the cop was on trial for being a crook. And out the window went the state's hope of a conviction.

A week after the trial, when the madam and the girls were back in business at the old stand, they sent Darrow a dozen American Beauty roses.

Some students of Clarence Seward Darrow are of the opinion that, all things considered, the man lived his shining hours in the summer of 1923 when, at the age of sixty-six, he appeared in the village of Dayton, the seat of Rhea County, in the Cumberland hills of Tennessee, as chief counsel for the defense in what the newspapers were to call the Monkey Trial. For it was in the Monkey Trial that Darrow, fighting against the bigoted opponents of man's right to think for himself, let go with a round-house wallop from which they have not, to this day, come up off the floor.

The state of Tennessee had passed a law which made it a crime for any schoolteacher to teach evolution, which adheres to the Darwin theory that man is allied biologically to the apes and monkeys. The proponents of the antimonkey law held that the Bible was to be taken literally: that Eve was made out of Adam's rib, that God made the world in six days, and that Jonah was swallowed by the whale. Although many religious men believed then, as they do today, that such statements in the Bible were not to be taken literally, but were only allegorical, certain brethren, called Fundamentalists, insisted that every statement in the Good Book was to be accepted as incontrovertible black-and-white fact.

So along came a young teacher in the high school of the town of Dayton, Tennessee—fellow named John T. Scopes—who believed in Darwin's theory rather than the theory of the Bible Fundamentalists. Scopes, a reddish-haired young man with the shyness, the eyeglasses, and the sober mien of the scholar, decided to put the antimonkey law to a test. He proceeded to tell his students that man was a cousin of the monkeys. And so he was arrested as a law violator and indicted.

William Jennings Bryan, the country's leading Fundamentalist and one of the most powerful and colorful figures of the era, had been the man behind passage of the antimonkey law. And so Bryan, a lawyer among his many other accomplishments, was naturally chosen to spearhead the prosecution of young Scopes. Since Bryan stood for everything that Darrow didn't stand for, Darrow did something he had never done in his life. He *asked* to get into a case. He said he would willingly go to Tennessee to defend Scopes, at his own expense, just to tangle with Bryan.

As Darrow saw the over-all picture, if Bryan wasn't defeated at the Scopes trial he would, through his nation-wide prestige, ram antimonkey laws through the legislatures of practically every state in the Union. That, as Darrow saw it, would be a mortal blow to freedom of thought.

The battle between Darrow and Bryan was to be a battle of two giants. Bryan—a big, bald-headed man with a benign countenance and golden voice—was a master spellbinder with a tremendous following. At the time of the Scopes trial, he was sixty-two, three years younger than Darrow. Starting out as a Missouri lawyer, he had embraced politics and, at the age of thirty-six, had so stirred the Democratic National Convention with his famous Cross of Gold speech that he had been nominated for the presidency. He ran on a platform of free and unlimited coinage of silver for the poor farmers and the poor workingmen and almost got into the White House. He ran again four years later, but was again defeated.

But Bryan, a tough adversary behind his benign exterior, was not through with politics—not by a country mile. At the Democratic Convention of 1912, he threw his weight behind Woodrow Wilson, and, as a result, broke a convention deadlock that got Wilson, an ex-Princeton professor and governor of New Jersey, the nomination and the presidency. Wilson appointed Bryan Secretary of State.

All the while, Bryan had been a lecturer on the Chautauqua Circuit, going out each year, grinding away at one cause or another. Always an opponent of drink, strong *or* weak, he began to stump for a prohibition law. He used to send out postal cards by the thousands, each bearing his signature, and requesting that the recipient sign his name above Bryan's. The catch was that above both signatures was a pledge that the recipient would never drink again. Darrow, getting hold of one of these postals once in awhile, would regard it sourly. "If I could only get enough of these," he once said, "I'd give them to some saloonkeeper so he could paper the toilet with them."

When, largely through Bryan's efforts, the Volstead Act was slipped into the nation's legal machinery like a Mickey in a drink, Bryan, ever the feverish guardian of his fellow man's welfare, began to cast an eye on any and all teaching that deviated from the literal truth of the Bible. He publicly offered a hundred dollars to anyone who could prove he was descended from an ape, and he embarked on a personal-appearance tour before legislatures in various parts of the country, pleading that the lawmakers pass statutes forbidding the teaching of evolution—or the Darwinian theory—in the public schools.

Bryan succeeded finally in ramming an antimonkey bill through the legislature of Tennessee. At first, nobody outside the state thought much about it. Then along came Scopes to join the issue between Bryan and Darrow.

Just as the trial of Bruno Richard Hauptmann for the murder of the Lindbergh baby turned the town of Flemington, New Jersey, into a three-ring circus, so did the monkey trial in Dayton, a decade earlier, convert that settlement into a big carnival. A couple of hundred reporters, both star and ordinary, all sorts of feature writers, and the flash-camera lads imposed a severe strain on Dayton hotel facilities and on the output of the local bootleggers.

Sidewalk preachers, most of them regional clerics but some from distant points, set up shop on the main street and shouted their exhortations from early morning until their voices gave out. At night, clusters of the faithful would go down to the river, and, out of their senses with religious fervor, jump into the waters and roll around, shouting hallelujahs.

The presiding judge at the trial—a little man named John Raulston—was a product of the Tennessee hills and a Fundamentalist all the way through. Darrow knew he wouldn't have an easy time.

The prosecution, with Bryan spearheading the attack, had pretty smooth sledding. Bryan established that Scopes had taught the theory that all life had begun in the sea and had, through the eons, assumed various forms until it emerged as man. While cross-examining Scopes, Bryan, a cagey old character, would leave the legal line to go off on a religious tangent, bringing cheers from the spectators and howls of disapproval from Darrow.

Darrow, sitting in his shirt sleeves and hitching his thumbs to a pair of bright scarlet suspenders bought especially for the trial, would, while listening to Bryan, scrutinize the courtroom spectators. One morning he riveted his gaze on a mountain boy who had such long hair that Darrow couldn't determine whether or not the lad's head came to a point on top. He nudged an associate counsel. "Take a good look at that fellow," he said. "If he's not proof that Darwin was right I hope never to leave this courtroom alive."

Darrow had lined up scientific men from all parts of the country to testify that there was scientific basis for Darwin's theory. Bryan fired his big gun when he objected to the introduction of such evidence—Darrow's most important evidence. The judge upheld the objection. Darrow blew a fuse. Then the judge blew one. Bryan looked on like a cat that had just finished a saucer of cream.

Darrow was cited for contempt. Next day, after he had cooled off, he apologized—as much, that is, as he was capable of apologizing. The judge accepted his apology and the trial resumed.

Now it was Darrow's turn to pull a fast one. He decided to execute a legal maneuver seldom seen in a courtroom. He called to the stand as a witness the chief counsel for the other side— William Jennings Bryan himself. The move made the lead headline in practically every newspaper in the land.

Darrow knew what he was doing. From the moment he had entered the Scopes case, he had assigned researchers to go into Bryan's past. Thus he knew that while Bryan was an authority on many subjects, he had only a sketchy knowledge of ancient history and science. He knew, too, that Bryan's forebears had been devout Fundamentalists and that Bryan, having been steeped in Fundamentalism since birth, had never so much as researched a single statement in the Bible.

So there was Bryan, up there on the stand, waving a palm-leaf fan to protect himself from the midsummer heat, and Darrow, in shirt sleeves and red suspenders, about to begin his attempt to take him apart.

Darrow got right down to the fundamental of Fundamentalism. He asked Bryan if he believed that Jonah had been swallowed by a whale. Bryan said he did. And did Brother Bryan believe that Joshua had made the sun stand still? Brother Bryan did.

"Do you know how long ago the Flood was—the Flood mentioned in the Bible?"

"Yes," said Bryan. "Two thousand, three hundred and forty-eight years B.C."

Bryan looked very confident. But then Darrow inquired whether Bryan knew that a number of civilizations dated back to more than 5,000 years before the birth of Christ—that the ancient civilizations of China were at least 6,000 or 7,000 years old. Bryan appeared puzzled. He had never studied up on such civilizations. Nor had he studied up on geology. Then he regained his ground and made a crack that is still good today. "I am, Mr. Darrow," he said, "more interested in the Rock of Ages than in the age of rocks."

Darrow scowled. Now he asked Bryan if he had ever made any attempt to learn how many people there had been in China 6,000 years ago. "No," came the answer. "And you, Mr. Darrow, are the first man I have ever met who has had any interest in the subject."

Darrow looked shocked. Did Bryan mean to say, he inquired, that he, Darrow, was the first man Bryan had ever met who had been interested in geology and primitive man? Bryan said he had meant to say precisely that. Darrow turned to look at the spectators. Then, turning back to Bryan, he asked, "Where, sir, have you been all your life?"

"Not," roared Bryan, "near *you*."

It went on and on, for hour after hour in the stifling heat of midsummer Tennessee. Bryan's answers were solid and sure-fire when they had anything to do with a statement anywhere in the Bible. But when Darrow asked him to back up some of the statements in the light of modern knowledge and science, Bryan just sat there, looking, for the first time in his life, completely stumped.

As the questioning went on, Darrow played with Bryan like a cat with a mouse. Regardless of the outcome of the trial itself, Darrow knew that he had Bryan where he wanted him. Bryan was game all the way through, but, for the first time in his life, he had met more than his equal in an argument. The trouble was he just didn't know the answers to the questions Darrow asked about evolution and science. When the questioning came to an end, Darrow was daisy-fresh. Bryan was soaked with perspiration and looked like a very old man.

Darrow knew what the verdict would be before it was brought in. But he knew something else: the press had been on his side and the American public at large—excepting, of course, the Fundamentalists—had come to regard the Tennessee anti-evolution statute as something ridiculous, not to be repeated in their own communities, and had in its collective mind a picture of William Jennings Bryan as a top-drawer bigot.

And so, when the jury brought in a verdict of guilty—that Scopes had taught evolution against a state statute—Darrow was not in the least surprised. The verdict had by now become comparatively unimportant. What was important was that Darrow's handling of the case had awakened the country to an existing evil. The bigots, led by Bryan or his successor, would never now be able to make it a national crime to teach evolution in the public schools.

Scopes was fined $100 by the judge; the verdict was to be reversed by the State Supreme Court on technical grounds, and the case was never to be retried.

Bryan hung around Dayton after the trial was over. Many men who don't drink liquor become gluttons. Bryan was such a man. He drowned his sorrow over his loss of the verbal battle in food. He sat down one steaming morning to a breakfast consisting of a large stack of hot cakes drenched in syrup, half a dozen fried eggs, three thick slabs of ham, a couple of pounds of fried potatoes, seven corn muffins, and six cups of coffee with cream and sugar. Then William Jennings Bryan laid down and died.

Darrow, who had gone to the mountains for a few days before returning to Chicago, took the news of Bryan's death quite calmly.

"They say that Mr. Bryan died of a broken heart," a reporter said to Darrow, "and that you were the cause of it."

Darrow snorted. "Broken heart, hell," he said. "He died of a busted belly."

Darrow was asleep in his Chicago apartment one night in the beginning of June, 1924, when he was awakened by the arrival of four hysterical visitors—relatives of two poor little rich boys who had just confessed to one of the most heartless murders in the history of American crime. Richard (Dickie) Loeb and Nathan Leopold, Jr., sons of two of Chicago's wealthiest and most illustrious families, had, for a thrill, kidnaped and murdered a 14-year-old boy named Bobby Franks and then attempted to collect ransom on the corpse.

The city, and then the entire country, was genuinely

shocked. Leopold, nineteen, tall and darkly handsome, and Loeb, small of stature and not very good-looking, came from a gold-plated environment. They drove around in foreign cars, carried hundred dollar bills in their pockets, kicked servants around, abused waiters in the tony spots, and did everything else that spoiled kids could possibly do. Surfeited with life, they had become queeries. Finally, looking for even another kind of thrill, they had cooked up a kidnaping and murder.

The leader of the visitors to Darrow's home that night was an uncle of Dickie Loeb. "Clarence," he said, "the families of the boys have authorized me to offer you one hundred thousand dollars if you can save the lives of Dickie and Nathan. That's all we ask of you—to save them from hanging. We realize that nothing more can be done." The deal was: ten thousand dollars down and the rest when the two necks were saved.

Whatever Darrow may have claimed publicly about Leopold and Loeb, he must have known, when he took the case, that they were a couple of young monsters. They had not the slightest remorse over what they had done. Worse, they seemed to be enjoying the black limelight that was beating down on them. "Bring us another kid," Leopold said to one of the jailors, "and we'll show you how we did it." Darrow was, purely and simply, out after that hundred-grand fee.

Darrow could smell danger. Thus it didn't take him very long to decide to plead the murderers guilty and avoid a jury trial. Had a jury had the slightest say in the matter, Leopold and Loeb would have swung as surely as the sun came up. They had committed not one but two offenses punishable by death—murder and kidnaping. So Darrow decided, in that instinctive way he had of measuring a situation, to put the entire responsibility for the fate on the killers on one man—the judge who would sentence them following their pleas of guilty.

A judge was, under his black robes, just as human as a juror or anyone else. Darrow knew from long experience that many a juror who had voted for a death penalty would not have done so had his decision alone decided the issue. But when there were eleven other men serving on a panel, a juror would be more likely to vote for the death penalty—especially in a case like this—because he would be only one-twelfth responsible, rather than wholly responsible, when the trap was sprung. But no judge, Darrow felt, relished the prospect of sentencing a person to death when he alone was making the decision and could just as easily sentence the defendant to life.

Now Darrow began to look around for the right kind of a judge for what he had in mind. A lawyer can't always get just the judge he wants, but sometimes he can find legitimate ways through the labyrinth of jurisprudence to get his man. So Darrow went to work behind the scenes and came up with Judge John Caverly—a brilliant and humane jurist. Now he was all set. He was ready to go into his act—an act that would culminate in a two-day speech designed to tear Judge Caverly's heart to shreds. There was just one thing to be done beforehand —make sure to keep Leopold and Loeb in line. The two killers were still smirking out loud, enjoying the whole business. "Now listen, you two," said Darrow. "Wipe those smiles off your faces when you go into that courtroom or they'll hang you, just as sure as hell."

Both sides produced alienists, as psychiatrists were called in those days—Darrow to indicate that his clients were just good boys at heart, the victims of unfortunate forces beyond their control, and the state of Illinois to point out that Leopold and Loeb were young fiends incarnate. Despite Darrow's warnings to his clients, and the tongue-lashings he gave them outside of the courtroom, Leopold and Loeb looked upon the court proceedings as a one-ring circus. They clowned and hammed through every session and the newspaper photographers caught them at it. Public opinion, strongly against the poor little rich boys at first, became stronger than ever. Courtroom spectators were revolted. Darrow was talking to himself. His clients were, in effect, insuring their own execution.

Now Darrow, his work cut out for him, began his summation. It was the same old story, new to every judge and jury who came under the Darrow spell. He began slowly, low and rich of voice, friendly of visage. He could feel the hostility in the courtroom, and in the judge. And then, somewhere along the line, that strange alchemy that happened to Clarence Darrow when the magic was upon him came to pass. Although he was sixty-seven, the years seemed to melt away. He was young and strong again and presently his words began to penetrate the hostility all around him. He was speaking not as a lawyer, try-ing to save the lives of two murderers, but as an apostle of good-ness, pleading that the judge, in all his wisdom, temper justice with mercy. He was representing not two murderers, but two boys who had taken a human life because they were mentally and morally sick, the victims of powerful, complicated, and un-seen forces that reached far back into time.

Darrow, a great believer in a certain school of thought among theatrical men that one way to achieve an effect on an audience is to exhaust it, had taken that tack now. His instincts told him, at the end of his first day of talking, that he had filled the judge with emotion. Now, as he began the second day, he decided to wring His Honor out. He went on and on about his two un-fortunate clients—victims of cosmic forces—now and then sneaking a look at them and, to himself, no doubt cursing the day they were born.

Why had Leopold and Loeb killed Bobby Franks after kidnaping him? Why, because of a perfectly ridiculous Illinois statute that he himself had fought against when it had been passed a few years before—the statute that made kidnaping an offense punishable by death. Why, these poor boys, these foolish, unfortunate boys, hadn't stopped to think, when they kidnaped Bobby Franks as a prank, that they were making themselves candidates for the noose. But then, when they realized that they had, in their childish, foolish way, committed an offense punishable by death, they had been driven by panic and thus had killed their victim so that he could not testify against them. Actually, then, Leopold and Loeb had been driven into a crime they would never have dreamed of committing by this foolish law that had made a boyish prank a capital offense.

That covered, Darrow went to work on the judge himself. The judge, he pointed out, was a fine man, a great jurist, a credit to all Chicago—remarks that could not help pleasing the listener. Surely, His Honor would not wish to cloud a distinguished career by sentencing these boys to die. "Your Honor," Darrow said, squinting at Judge Caverly, "if these two boys hang, *you* must order them to hang. It will be entirely up to *you*, Your Honor. There must be no division of responsibility here, Your Honor. The sentencing of these boys to die must be an act on *your* part and on your part alone. Such a sentencing must be your own cold, deliberate, premeditated act, without the slightest chance to shift any part of the responsibility. Your Honor alone stands between these boys and the trap door of the scaffold."

His Honor chose to duck the responsibility of sending those two poor boys to the scaffold. He gave them life imprisonment instead.

Now Darrow sat around his office waiting for the Leopold

and Loeb families to kick in with the ninety thousand dollars. Nothing happened. So he sent the paymaster for the families a gentle note. No answer. Another note . Still no answer. Another note. Another dose of silence. Darrow thought of suing. Then a fiscal agent for the two families appeared in his office with the fee, but in three checks of thirty thousand dollars each. Two other lawyers had assisted Darrow in the case and were entitled to some of the money but not, as Darrow saw it, to two-thirds of it. But rather than get into a public hassle about dough he settled on the terms of the Loeb and Leopold families. Ever afterward, when some newspaper reporter would interview him and ask him to talk about his celebrated cases, Darrow would duck the Leopold-Loeb case. Somehow, when he thought of it, he felt a headache coming on.

In the year of 1925, when Clarence Darrow was in the sixty-eighth year of his life, there came to pass a happening in Detroit that altered his plans to withdraw from the turmoil of the legal arena. There appeared in Detroit a young colored physician, a Dr. Ossian Sweet, with his wife and infant son. This Sweet was quite a man, in any color. Coming up from his native Florida where the cards had been stacked against him, he had become a bellhop on the lake steamers between Detroit and Chicago. Somehow he had got together enough money to pay his tuition through the medical school of Howard University in Washington. Then he had gone to Europe to study in Vienna and later to specialize in gynecology and pediatrics at the Curie Institute in France. Coming to Detroit, he practiced in a colored district where he became so renowned in his specialties that white patients frequently crossed the color line to avail themselves of his skill.

In 1925, Dr. Sweet moved to the corner of Charlevoix and Garland Streets, then a district of foreign-born workers. White residents threatened him. He appealed to the police. The Detroit Police Department, then honeycombed with Ku Kluxers, ignored him. Sweet sent his wife and baby away and, with his two brothers, Otis, a dentist, and Henry, a medical student, and eight friends, stocked up with ammunition and stood by for a battle.

One night a mob gathered outside and stoned and set fire to the house. The doctor was seriously injured by a rock. Now his younger brother—the one he was sending through medical school—let go with his rifle. A man in the mob fell dead. The cops pinched the eleven Negroes on a murder charge.

Called to defend them, Darrow hired tipsters to infiltrate the neighborhood of the violence and find out what they could. Meantime he went into seclusion and absorbed every piece of literature he could lay hands on relating to the history of the Negro. He traced the Negro people through the corridors of time from their earliest known beginnings up through the centuries right into Detroit. He became deeply stirred by the black man's long history of unjust treatment, tragedy, and oppression.

By now the tipsters had established pipelines right into the prosecutor's office. They learned that the prosecution was going to try to show that the shooting from within Dr. Sweet's house had been utterly unprovoked, that there had not been, in fact, any mob outside of the doctor's house. The doctor, the prosecution was going to contend, lived at a busy street intersection and although it may have been slightly more crowded than usual the night of the shooting, the people who were there were bent on ordinary pursuits, certainly not assembled with malice aforethought.

Now Darrow assigned his tipsters to knocking down the prosecution's case before it was really built up. They located several motorists who said that on the night of the shooting there had been such a large crowd around the Sweet home that the cops had to reroute traffic.

Darrow made hamburgers out of the state's witnesses—a sickening parade of first-degree perjurers, some of whom pictured the corner of Charlevoix and Garland Streets that night as having been about as crowded as Death Valley. Others represented themselves as hardy souls who had been abroad in the wilderness bent on locating stray pets. Darrow lay in wait, like a tiger, for the state's witnesses to finish their stories. Then he pounced on them and clawed them to ribbons.

Now Darrow put Dr. Sweet on the stand. The physician, like Darrow, had studied the history of the Negro; he had also studied the history of mob violence in which Negroes had been victims. He told of his inward terror of a certain type of white man ever since, during his days as a medical student in Washington, he had seen a crowd of supremists roaming the streets, in the very shadow of the White House, on the prowl for a Negro who had committed a crime. All of which established the state of mind of Dr. Sweet and the ten other Negroes in the house when the mob begun to stone the place.

Darrow had probed into the past of the jurors. Several of the jurors selected by the state whom he had been unable to block were Ku Kluxers. That meant the best Darrow could hope for was a disagreement. So, in his summation he addressed his remarks to two jurors who, his scouts had learned, hated Ku Kluxer. He got his disagreement.

Now the state tried young Henry Sweet—the fellow who had actually fired the shot—alone. Again Darrow found a couple of jurors who were opposed to the Kluxers. There was a third juror he couldn't quite make up his mind about. When the jury was filing out, the man looked at Darrow with a small enigmatic smile on his face. "I would give ten years of my life," Darrow whispered to an assistant, "to know how that fellow is going to vote." It was to work out that the little man with the enigmatic smile turned on the smile again when he reached the jury room with his fellow jurors. He had brought with him a box of nickel cigars.

"I'm going to smoke these," he said to the foreman. "You and the others go ahead and talk things over. I'll just be sitting in the corner there, smoking."

"But," said the foreman, "you've got to consider the evidence with us."

"I don't need to consider it," said the smiling man. "My mind's made up. When the rest of you have agreed to acquit, I'll vote your way."

The verdict was acquittal for Henry Sweet. Then the state dismissed the charges against his two brothers and the other defendants. The Sweet case became a legal and civic milestone in the Negro people's progress in the twentieth-century United States—one that is still talked about in the law schools.

Darrow hated prohibition. Once, while lecturing against it in a Chicago suburb, he spotted Al Capone in the audience. He knew what Capone had come for. Not, certainly, to hear him speak against the evils of prohibition, but to size him up as a possible mouthpiece. Darrow had heard that the T-Men—the Treasury sleuths—had come to Chicago to dig up evidence on Capone as an income-tax violator, everything else having failed to trap the Big Boy. Capone would thus be in need of top-grade legal assistance. It would be natural for the gangster, loaded as he was, to seek out the best talent to be had.

Sure enough, Darrow was visited in his office a couple of days later by a sharply dressed fellow whose eyes were a day's march from his cheekbones.

"The Boss would like to see you, Mr. Darrow," said the visitor.

Darrow, shuffling some papers, didn't look up. "You mean Capone?" he asked.

"Yeah," said the visitor.

"I'm not interested in seeing Capone," said Darrow.

"But he says you can name your own figure, Mr. Darrow—anything."

Now Darrow looked up. He said, "Capone is helping to ruin this whole country with that stuff of his that is being sold to nice decent kids. You go back and tell the sonofabitch that there ain't enough money in the world for me to have anything to do with him."

In the late Twenties, Darrow and his wife went to Europe. When they came back he decided he'd had enough of the law. He had invested his Leopold-Loeb money in the market and seemed to be pretty well fixed. He settled down to reading, writing pamphlets, and lecturing occasionally for causes he favored, and just loafing.

Then, in 1929, when Darrow was seventy-two, he was practically wiped out financially by the stock-market crash. He began to take cases again—practically any kind of case. He established connections in Washington and began to represent racketeers who had fallen afoul of the income-tax statutes. He went into court and got a few murderers off—or at least got them prison jolts instead of the noose. He was in a pretty bad way.

Darrow had reached his seventy-fifth year when, in 1932, he found himself suddenly stimulated by front-page newspaper stories coming out of Honolulu. Lieutenant Thomas H. Massie of the submarine service of the United States Navy, stationed at Pearl Harbor, and his wife, Thalia, went to a drink-and-dance affair at a night club one hot night and during the course of the evening got into one of those husband-and-wife spats usually forgotten in the morning.

Mrs. Massie, an attractive woman of twenty-three, some four years her husband's junior, decided to leave the party and walk home alone. It was around midnight. In the course of her walk, she was obliged to traverse the same route as that taken by local prostitutes catering to servicemen in the district. Mrs. Massie was halfway home when a car drew up and she was abducted by five men. She was driven to a remote spot and raped by all five. The girl's assailants she described as being a Hawaiian and four men apparently of mixed breed.

From the very beginning, this was more than just another rape case—vicious and depraved though rape is in itself. This was a *race* case. The racial problem in the islands had begun long years previously when, according to the way Darrow later put it, the white man had come to Hawaii, taught the yellow and brown men to look upward to pray, and then, when the prayer was finished and the yellow and brown men looked down again, their land had been stolen from them.

There were, in the Honolulu police department, some Orientals who didn't see much, if anything, wrong with what the five men had done to the white woman. In the twelve months prior to the attack on Thalia Massie, almost fifty native women in and near Honolulu had been raped by United States sailors, who were apparently not in a position to pay for their fun, and some of the women had been hospitalized. So the investigation into the attack on Mrs. Massie was being kicked around in the hope that it would get lost in the shuffle when the resident Navy brass and the white population demanded, and got, effective action.

The five rapists were arrested and quickly identified by Mrs.

Massie. The leader of the gang was a bad egg by the name of Joe Kahahawai who was none the less a local hero because of his all-around athletic prowess; the four others were of Hawaiian, Japanese, and Chinese ancestry.

The case against the five men was tried before an all-Oriental jury. What was expected to happen happened. The jury couldn't agree on a verdict and the five blackguards were released until such time as they might be tried again.

Lieutenant Massie, a Virginian, and his mother-in-law—Mrs. Granville Fortescue, a haughty society dowager with moxie to spare—cooked up a little plot. Together with two sailors—fellows named Jones and Lord—Massie picked Kahahawai, the athlete, off a downtown street and drove him to a bungalow that had been rented by Mrs. Fortescue. There the two sailors pinioned Kahahawai against a wall while Massie, pointing a revolver at the culprit, demanded that he spill his story.

The Hawaiian spoke just four words: "Yeah, we done it." Massie fired one shot—practically involuntarily, Darrow was to claim—and killed the Hawaiian.

Massie and the two sailors wrapped up the body and dumped it in Mrs. Fortescue's car. Leaving one of the sailors behind in the bungalow to clean up the blood, the others headed for a promontory where they could throw the corpse into the sea. Meantime, however, the cops had gotten wind that Kahahawai had been kidnaped and they were on the prowl for the abductors. Thus the law overtook Mrs. Fortescue's car before its occupants had a chance to dispose of the corpse.

When Lieutenant Massie, Mrs. Fortescue, and the two sailors were charged with murder, the cleavage between the whites and those of the other races in Hawaii widened and deepened. Since there were roughly ten Orientals to every white man in Honolulu, the jury that would sit at the trial of the four defendants would be preponderantly Oriental. And since the murder victim had been an Oriental, even a moron would not be puzzled if asked to prognosticate the verdict.

Clarence Darrow got a telephone call from a representative of the Fortescue family. The caller wanted Darrow to go to Hawaii to represent the four defendants. "We will pay all your expenses, Mr. Darrow," said the caller, "and we are perfectly willing to pay you a fee of twenty-five thousand dollars in advance." Darrow took it on.

As Darrow saw the problem, even from the distance, the Massie case would stand or fall on an emotional rather than a legal level. By the time he landed in Hawaii, the four defendants had been indicted by an all-white grand jury, not for murder, but for second-degree murder. The lessened degree of the offense that had been decided upon by the white grand jurors only added fuel to the already roaring fire of resentment among the Oriental population.

Darrow got six white men on the jury. So he felt at the outset that the worst he would achieve would be an even break—a disagreement. In distilling the whole case to its fundamentals he concluded that the law was on the side of the prosecution and that life, and the human qualities that preserve it, were on his side. This was, as Darrow later put it, a conflict between the dead letter of the law and the living emotions upon which all life rests.

And so, deciding to pull out every last emotional stop, he put the defendants on the stand. There was no conflict in the evidence; nothing was to be denied. Instead, the defendants were to dwell on the emotional reasons for what they had done. The two sailors, for example, had acted out of loyalty to their superior officer. The husband had gone temporarily insane when the leader of the men who had ravaged his wife looked right at him and admitted what he had done. Mrs. Fortescue had acted out of mother love, the strongest instinct in the animal kingdom.

Mrs. Massie herself took the stand. She not only told of the attack. She told how the attackers had made her pregnant and that she had had to have an abortion performed.

When Darrow began his summation, after five weeks of the trial, he was an old and haggard man. As he moved into his task—a task that was to consume four hours—that same strange thing happened that had more than once happened before. The lines seemed to vanish from his face, and the ravages of age appeared to be lifted from his bent shoulders. His voice, cracked up to now, was somehow suddenly mended. He hitched his thumbs in his suspenders and ambled up and down in front of the jurors. He felt that the white men were with him. He concentrated his remarks on the Orientals in the box. He pleaded not only for his clients but for all humanity in the Hawaiian islands. He asked for justice among the white and the brown and the yellow men, for an end to the cancerous internal strife.

His voice was high and low, by turn harsh and mellow. He was the maestro of old, playing on the human emotions. And then, toward the end of the four hours, a curious transformation occurred. The years suddenly came back and enveloped him, lining his face, bending his back and cracking his voice. He was to say later that he suddenly realized that he was not going to get an acquittal. He saw in the faces of the Orientals on the jury the fathomless mysteries of the Orient. "I knew," he said to an associate counsel, "that I was not registering on those bastards."

The jury was out for two days. It brought in a verdict of manslaughter, with a recommendation for mercy. The judge handed each of the four defendants a ten-year jolt in prison.

But Darrow had so raised a storm of public opinion, principally by putting Mrs. Massie on the stand, that the governor, not a bad judge of public opinion, commuted the ten-year sentences to one hour.

Now came an unusual development. The prosecuting authorities—the very authorities Darrow had just beaten—asked him to come over to their side and help prosecute the four living men who had assaulted Mrs. Massie. For anybody but Darrow such a request would have posed no dilemma. Here he was being given a chance to mete out justice to the men whose reprehensible actions had brought about the situation he had just defended. But Darrow didn't have to think long in order to decide about the request.

"No thanks," he said. "I've been defending people for half a century and I don't intend to start prosecuting them now."

As a matter of fact, Darrow talked the Massies into dropping their charges against the four attackers.

The Massie affair was his last big trial. Except for a few small scattered cases, his courtroom career was over.

Clarence Darrow died in March 1938, near the end of his eighty-first year. For two days and two nights people passed his bier in a Chicago funeral parlor—including ex-clients, clients, and prospective clients. Detectives kept an eye on the mourners. More than one of them was picked up. One dip, whom Darrow had once defended, was caught in the act of relieving a fat man of his wallet.

WILLIAM JOSEPH FALLON

One fine day back in the Twenties, a meek-looking little man walked into the law offices of Fallon and McGee at Times Square, New York City, desperately in need of legal advice. Consulting William Joseph Fallon, then the greatest criminal lawyer in the country, he divulged that he was a teller in one of the city's largest banks, that he had gambled and lost ten thousand dollars of the bank's money in the stock market, and that the bank examiners, due any day, would be certain to find him out.

"I'm afraid I'll be sent to prison, Mr. Fallon," said the meek little man. "I've read a lot about you in the papers and I was wondering if there was anything you could do to keep me out of prison. I've got a wife and family and the disgrace to them would be something awful."

"You say you stole ten thousand dollars," said Fallon.

"That's right, Mr. Fallon."

"How much more can you get?" asked Fallon.

The prospective client didn't exactly understand the question.

"I say," repeated Fallon, "how much more can you get? How much more can you lay hands on?"

"You mean how much more can I *steal?*"

"If you want to put it that way, yes."

"Oh, I could get practically any amount, I guess. But I don't understand why you should ask me that."

"Could you get fifty thousand dollars and be back here with it before the examiners get there?"

"Oh, sure. I could get practically any amount, I guess. But I don't want to take any more. God, Mr. Fallon, I'm in enough trouble already."

"You just do as I say," said Fallon. "Be here as quick as you can with the fifty thousand dollars and I'll guarantee to keep you out of jail. Otherwise you're sure to go."

The little man didn't understand it. If he was in deep trouble because he had stolen ten thousand dollars, why wouldn't he be in deeper trouble if he ran his take up to sixty thousand dollars? Fallon grew impatient. His client could follow his advice—or else.

Next day the little man appeared with the fifty thousand dollars. Fallon counted the money, then told his client to register at a certain hotel under an assumed name and lie low until he heard from him. Then Fallon telephoned to the president of the bank. He was short and sweet. "You're sixty thousand dollars short in your accounts," he informed the banker. "I represent the teller who took the money. I think I can recover forty thousand dollars of it for you if you agree not to prosecute."

The banker was outraged at the proposition. But when he thought it over and weighed both sides of the problem, he decided that it wasn't worth forty thousand dollars to send the teller to prison and get his bank a heap of bad publicity to boot. So a few days later he phoned Fallon and agreed to the deal. By this time Fallon had begun to feel a little sorry for the thief. The man had been working for the bank since he left grammar school and was still getting coolie wages. "You'll not only agree not to prosecute," Fallon told the banker, "but you'll give my client a fine recommendation so that he can get another job somewhere."

The banker, having no other course, agreed to that, too. So Fallon returned the forty thousand dollars, pocketed the remaining ten thousand dollars and got rid of it within a week by hitting the hot spots and buying a couple of automobiles for lady friends.

That's a story that's been going the rounds these many years about William J. Fallon, the great mouthpiece. It is in all probability true, for it would have been typical of Fallon. He was the trickiest, cleverest, shadiest big-time criminal lawyer New York has ever known, and the big burg has had a few. Fallon, in fact, rates with the celebrated courtroom strategists in all American criminal history—right up there with Clarence Darrow of Chicago and Earl Rogers of Los Angeles.

Fallon, a stalwart redhead who dripped with magnetism, could charm a bird out of a tree, let alone a lady into a hotel room. He wanted no truck with dry legal cases; the colorful criminal stuff was his meat. He defended gunmen, gangsters, prohibition racketeers, income-tax evaders, such underworld big shots as Arnold Rothstein, and such glamor pusses as Peggy Hopkins Joyce, who once got in trouble with the customs people for forgetting to declare a bagful of diamonds that she had brought in from Europe.

Legends spring up about lawyers and if the lawyers are smart they capitalize on the legends. The legend that fastened itself to Bill Fallon was that the worst that could happen to a client of his was a hung jury—eleven for conviction and one for acquittal. Then the case would be retried and retried and finally kicked around until it got lost.

The story along the Broadway grapevine was that Fallon,

acting through underworld intermediaries, bought off the twelfth juror in a tough case. He sometimes denied this. "Most jurors are dumb," he once told Fanny Brice, when he was hiding her husband, Nicky Arnstein, from the law. "All I have to do is to pick out the dumbest of the dozen, concentrate everything on him, and my client is sure of a hung jury."

By concentrating everything, Fallon meant more than the evidence. Sometimes the prosecution had evidence so damaging to Fallon's client that Fallon was obliged to divert attention from it. On such occasions, *he* became the defendant, rather than the man who was on trial. He deliberately did things that brought the wrath of the prosecutor and the judge down upon him, then turned that wrath to his advantage.

Once, for example, he was cross-examining a detective who was the state's star witness against a crook client. The questioning began in normal enough fashion, with Fallon speaking in a moderate tone of voice and standing a respectful distance from the witness. As the cross-examination progressed, Fallon's voice grew louder and he inched closer to the witness until he was practically in the man's lap and shouting at the top of his voice.

The district attorney, speaking in a normal tone, told the judge he objected to Fallon's tone of voice. Fallon kept right on shouting at the witness. Now the judge banged his gavel so hard he almost broke it and instructed Fallon to stop talking. Fallon, not taking his eyes from the witness, kept right on shouting. Now the judge began to shout at Fallon. Finally Fallon turned to His Honor, cupped a hand to his ear, and inquired if the judge was talking to him.

"*Yes*, I'm talking to you!" shouted the judge. "What did Your Honor say?" asked Fallon.

"I said I'm talking to you," roared the judge, "and instructing you not to stand so close to the witness and shout at him." Fallon cupped his hand to his ear again and stood there looking puzzled. "What did Your Honor say?" Now the judge began to roar even louder. Fallon looked startled, then hung his head. He couldn't, he said, help it if he had recently suffered an injury that had impaired his hearing. "You mean you are deaf?" asked the judge. Fallon couldn't hear the man. The judge roared a repetition of his question, "Yes, Your Honor," said Fallon, looking at the jury out of the corner of his eye. "I fear that I may never be able to hear normally again."

For the balance of the trial, poor Fallon had to shout at the state's witnesses and practically sit in their laps while the prosecutor and the judge had to interrupt him frequently. "Your Honor," said the prosecutor, "I think counsel is only pretending he is deaf." Fallon asked the judge what the man had said. The judge shouted the information. Fallon looked sad again. "Would that I were but pretending," he said.

The jury was obviously touched by Fallon's plight. Fallon didn't put the defendant on the stand because, he, not the crook, had become the defendant. And of course the crook was acquitted.

Outside the courtroom after the verdict was in, Fallon tapped the prosecutor on the shoulder. "Pardon me, sir," he whispered, "but if I'm not mistaken I heard you drop a pin back there."

No less an authority than David Belasco, the great theatrical producer, who was a close friend of Fallon's thought that Fallon had missed his true destiny when he took up law instead of acting. In Belasco's considered opinion, Fallon would have made a great tragedian. There was something tragic about his square, Hibernian face, something wistful in his China-blue eyes, and he was born to the dramatic gesture. His voice had a rich, throbbing timbre not unlike that of his friend John Barrymore but he didn't always have to use it to produce an effect.

He could cock his head and convey more anger or surprise than a pedestrian prosecutor could with a thousand words and when, in the midst of a fiery exchange with a reluctant witness, he would abruptly stop talking, hunch his shoulders and hang his head, he was as tragic as Hamlet learning the truth about his father's death.

Fallon was at his dramatic best in the summer of 1924 when, after being tried in federal court for jury bribing, he summed up his own case. His ancient enemy, William Randolph Hearst, had instigated the charge and the evidence against Fallon seemed so completely and utterly damning that Fallon's lawyer could do little to rebut it. There was only one thing to do, and that was for Bill Fallon to plead his own case by summing up to the jury.

Thus it was that on a steaming morning Fallon got up to begin his address to the jurors—the address that he hoped would save his legal life. Dressed in a finely cut blue-serge suit and wearing a burgandy necktie, he was, more than ever, Hamlet in a tragic hour. He talked in low tones, with sweet reasonableness, and he talked not so much about the evidence that the prosecution had presented, but about life in general and about his own life in particular. He had only gotten into his summation, if it could be called that, when there was a break for lunch.

"That was a dumb thing to do, Bill," his counsel told him as the jurors went out to lunch, "breaking up your summation like that. The whole effect of the thing will be lost while they're out eating."

"On the contrary," said Fallon. "I've planted the seed. It will grow while they're out stuffing themselves at government expense."

And so in the afternoon the jurors came back, well fed and looking very interested in what Fallon had to say. He took up where he had left off, pacing up and down, addressing his remarks first to this juror, then to that one. He was, that steaming day in July of 1924, not a lawyer addressing a jury but, rather, an actor performing before an audience.

Once in a while he would supply a little comedy to relieve the tension—some anecdote about his early life as a lawyer, how unresourceful he had been on certain occasions. As the sun sank lower in the white-hot sky, Fallon became more and more the underdog. He spoke of his mother—his dear sainted mother —and he whipped a snow-white handkerchief from his breast pocket and dabbed at his eyes. He spoke of his days at Fordham Law School, when he had had dreams of becoming a great lawyer—for his dear old mother's sake. He told the jurors how, in his early days as a prosecutor in Westchester County, New York, he had once, in his zeal to do his job, sent an innocent man to prison—without knowing it, of course—and how, ever after that he had been dedicated to seeing that there would never be another miscarriage of justice if he could do anything about it.

But of course he had made mistakes in his life, Fallon told the jurors. To err, he pointed out, was human; to forgive divine. The judge interrupted him at this point. He instructed an attendant to show a woman out of the courtroom. It was all right to cry, but this woman was practically wailing.

And so it came to pass that late in the afternoon William Joseph Fallon came to the end of his summation. He ceased his walking and stood in the center of the jury box. He tilted his head slightly upward and he outstretched his arms in supplication. "Gentlemen of the jury," he said, in a voice lowered almost to a whisper, "all that is dear to me, all that life means to me, I now place in your hands." His arms dropped to his sides and he lowered his head until his chin rested on his chest. Thus he stood, completely motionless, for fully thirty seconds.

And so the jury filed out to decide upon the fate of William Joseph Fallon. There was no doubt in the minds of anybody, even Fallon's friends, that he had been guilty of purchasing a juror. The big question along the Broadway grapevine was: had Fallon succeeded, once more, in making the jury forget the evidence and, by his own dramatic charm, sold it a bill of goods? The verdict this time was the most important one of Bill Fallon's life. For if the verdict was guilty, the great mouthpiece would not only be finished; he would go to prison.

The whole town was pulling for Fallon because the man was indeed a beloved rogue. Headwaiters and bellhops loved him because he threw money around like confetti. Practically every rooter for the New York Giants followed the Fallon bribery trial in the papers as if it were a World Series because Fallon was one of the town's top Giant rooters and a close friend of John J. McGraw, the Giant manager. Politicians, society figures, and mobsters were offering Jack Doyle, Broadway's betting commissioner, 6 to 5 that Fallon would get at least a hung jury—and not one he hung himself. Fallon didn't let them down. . . .

Although Fallon was married, and had been for twelve years, he didn't work at it. He had a wife who was part human, part angel. Whenever, after flying long and high he came home to roost, she never so much as asked him where he had been or what he had been doing, probably because she knew the answers in advance and because she simply loved the big fellow.

Fallon's partner, Eugene McGee, was several years older than he, and had frequently lectured at Fordham Law School when Fallon was a student there. The firm of Fallon and McGee was known as the Broadway and Forty-second Street Bar Association. McGee did the research on a case and handed it over to

Fallon. Then Fallon would dramatize the research in the courtroom.

The Broadway and Forty-second Street Bar Association operated on strictly a cash basis, except when the client was a
pretty woman. Then Fallon would refuse to accept any money.
"Gosh, Bill," McGee complained one day when Fallon refused
to take a fee from a chorus girl who had come in to be defended
for assaulting a woman who had caught her with her husband,
"we've got to eat." "How can you think of food, Gene," coun-
tered Fallon, "when you look at anything as beautiful as that?"

Both Fallon and McGee were late sleepers, not usually getting into the office until late morning or early afternoon unless
there was a big trial going on. Although they took in elaborate
sums, they had a crummy office and just one secretary. The
secretary would accept retainers from prospective clients who
called when neither of the partners was in. Many mornings the
secretary would collect one or more retainers, often totalling
two or three thousand dollars, and put the money in a tin box.
Whichever of the partners arrived for work first rifled the box.
Sometimes Fallon got the money and sometimes McGee got it.

Although Fallon and McGee were for all practical purposes
robbing each other, they never had so much as a loud word
about these trips to the till. It was all part of the game. Anyway,
the larcenies were about evenly divided between the two men.
A friend once asked Fallon if he thought McGee was getting
the better of him by this unique method of dividing the spoils.

"Not at all," said Fallon. "In fact, we're both better off because of it. It saves bookkeeping."

Apparently, neither Fallon nor McGee ever made the slightest effort to beat one another to the morning's bag unless they
just happened to arrive in the vicinity of Broadway and Forty-
second Street about the same time. Then, spotting one another,

they would, instead of greeting each other as partners, begin a race to the office. Since each man tossed it away at night, he was usually flat in the morning. The last one in would usually have to borrow fifty or a hundred dollars from the other—until the next day. The next day never arrived.

McGraw, the manager of the Giants, who was one of Fallon's drinking companions, once asked him why he didn't dispense with McGee and go it alone. "John," said Fallon, "every comedian would be dead without a straight man. I'm a comedian and Gene's a straight man."

Although Bill Fallon had the generosity of a drunken sailor in most things, such as buying gems and automobiles for his lady friends and handing out big tips, there was an impecunious side to his nature. He shined his own shoes, cut his own hair, and, when escorting a handsomely attired lady to her diggings after an evening on the town, always rode the subway or street cars, never in a taxi.

Belasco, the sage of the make-believe world, once asked him about these apparently stingy traits. Fallon, never at a loss for an explanation, explained that he thought it was degrading for a man to be a bootblack and that he didn't want to contribute to the degradation of anybody. He offered Belasco the same explanation for cutting his own hair, although the general opinion was that Fallon had such a handsome shock of the stuff that he didn't want to take a chance on any barber cutting it improperly. So far as his refusal to use taxis went, he insisted that he considered them dangerous. "Just look at all the accidents taxis get into," he would say. "You never hear of street cars and subway trains getting into trouble like that. Anyhow, subways are faster and you see such interesting people in them."

In his later years, in the days before he went on trial for jury bribing, Fallon became a real drunk, an authentic lush. His devotion to liquor, however, never seemed to take the edge off his sharp mind, and it never road-blocked his way to a court-room when the chips were down. Fallon did, however, fre-quently appear in the august portals of justice with whisky on his breath. After a night on the town he would often have only enough time to shave, take a bath, and change his clothes before grabbing a quick breakfast and hustling off to court. In his later years, Fallon's breakfast more often than not consisted of a couple of raw eggs dropped in half a tumblerful of rye. That would carry him through to the noon recess when he would repeat the nourishment—often without the eggs.

One morning, down in the old Criminal Courts Building on Centre Street, near Police Headquarters, Fallon appeared before a straight-laced judge to argue for a reduction of bail for a client. Fallon was in particularly good form that morning and his words had wings. But the judge didn't seem so intent on what Fallon was saying as on sniffing the air around him. Finally His Honor leaned forward, fixed Fallon with a severe stare, and inquired, "Is it possible that counsel has been drinking?"

Fallon blinked, smiled warmly, stepped back a few feet, and bowed from the waist. "If," he said, "Your Honor's sense of justice is as keen as Your Honor's sense of smell, I shall have no fear that my client's bail will be reduced."

The judge was completely enchanted. As he smiled, he seemed to be fighting back the desire to laugh out loud. He sat back and told Fallon to proceed with his argument. The bail was reduced.

William Joseph Fallon was that *rara avis*—a native New Yorker. He was born in the home of his parents—Joseph and Mary Fallon, natives of Ireland—in a handsome four-story red brick house in the two-hundred block of West Forty-seventh Street. Fallon, senior, though under thirty when Willie was born, ran a highly successful market. He had already been blessed with two daughters, not entirely to his satisfaction, since he preferred boys. Willie Fallon's mother was a gentle, retiring woman, but the old man was a belligerent character. "What the hell use is a girl in a corner street fight?" he used to inquire of neighbors. "Why, she can't de*fend* herself." So the drinks were on Old Man Fallon on January 23, 1886, when Willie, the first of two sons, checked in.

When a couple of years after Willie's birth, the second son came along, making a family of six, not counting a couple of servants, Old Man Fallon decided to get out of Manhattan, out somewhere in the country where the air was fresh and there was room to move around. So the Fallons sold the red-brick house on West Forty-seventh Street and moved to Mamaroneck, on Long Island Sound, up in Westchester County. There the elder Fallon opened another market and the kids went to school.

Although there was always whisky around the house, it never occurred to Willie Fallon, as it does to so many boys, that he would drink the stuff when he grew up. If anything, he had the makings of an abstainer by the time he was ten years old. The smell of whisky practically nauseated him.

As Willie Fallon reached his teens, he began to worship his mother—something that he did to the end of his days. To him, there was no woman on earth like his mother, which was probably one reason why he was to make such a poor husband. Willie, as his mother and father always called him, was, despite his practically unnatural love for his mother, a boy's boy— handy with his fists and good at sports. Girls never interested him. He was, in fact, shy in their presence—something of a Ripley considering what a wow he later became with them.

Fallon's mother wanted him to become a priest so he began to study at Fordham University in New York City. But by the time he had completed his regular college course, the ham in him cropped out. He thought of going on the stage and becoming a great star but he knew that such a course would break the heart of his mother. The next best thing, then, was the law. Stalwart, handsome, and with a lightning mind and a golden voice, he could picture himself strutting before juries, spellbinding them in the cause of justice. Fallon's parents, his mother in particular, had always stressed the terrible wages of sin. God was on the side of the just—and it was with that in mind that Fallon began the study of law at Fordham.

Eugene McGee, a big, rough-hewn young Irishman who was already practicing law in Manhattan, frequently did special teaching at Fordham. McGee was quick to recognize in Fallon a future whiz at the bar. Came graduation day and McGee approached Fallon. "Bill," he said, "why don't you come in with me as a junior partner? We would be a great success together."

Fallon wasn't interested. For one thing, he didn't want to go to New York. His mother had begun to picture him as practicing, preferably as a prosecutor, up in Westchester County. So Fallon opened up a little office in White Plains, the county seat. He was twenty-three at the time. He didn't find private practice as exciting as he had hoped it would be. For one thing, there weren't many exciting cases—mostly dry legal stuff.

Still worshipping his mother, Fallon never bothered with girls. Until, that is, he was twenty-six. Then he met a girl named Agnes Rafter—an Irish colleen who reminded him of his mother. Agnes' father ran a chain of grocery stores. She and Fallon were married at the Church of the Holy Trinity in New York City in June of 1912.

Agnes thought it would be fine if her young and handsome husband ran for the state legislature. Dreamer that she was, she pointed out that if he got into politics he might someday become governor. So he went around making speeches and his charm got him elected.

Up in Albany, Fallon was distressed to find himself among a bunch of political hacks and windbags who were pumping for a lot of legislation that was, to him anyway, as dull as the law books. So he sat out most of his term back in White Plains. But by now the Fallon charm had attracted quite a bit of local attention. The fellow was not only brilliant and handsome but witty and winning. The district attorney of Westchester County, a fine public servant named Frederick E. Weeks, decided that Fallon was just the boy he needed on his staff—the boy to handle the tough ones with juries. So Fallon was appointed Assistant District Attorney in 1914, when he was twenty-eight.

Prosecuting, with its opportunity for courtroom dramatics, suited Fallon just fine. All the tough cases—the ones the D.A. stood a fair chance of losing—were turned over to him. Young Fallon had an unerring instinct for finding the flaw in the story of a witness for the defense. And if there wasn't a flaw to be found, Fallon would create one. He seemed to take the position that the end justified the means. If he could, by trickery, trip up an obviously honest witness for the defense, he used trickery. Once, for example, he was cross-examining a man who was testifying to the good character of a fellow charged with breaking into a home. At one stage of the testimony of the character witness, the man said that during the night of the robbery he had left his home to go out and buy a quart of milk.

"How long would you say you were out of your house going for that quart of milk?" asked Fallon.

"Maybe twenty minutes."

"How far from your house was the store where you bought that milk?"

"Three doors away."

"Yet it took you twenty minutes to buy that quart of milk?"

The witness nodded.

"Was the store crowded so that you didn't get waited on for about twenty minutes?"

No, the store had been empty.

"Well, then, why did it take you twenty minutes?"

"I didn't go right to the store. I took a walk."

"Oh! So you didn't really go out to buy the milk at all. What you really went out for was a walk. May I ask where you went during that walk—and what the *real reason* was behind that walk?"

The witness began to squirm a little bit. He couldn't quite explain why he had taken such a roundabout course to buy a quart of milk. Fallon kept pressing the man for an explanation. The witness couldn't supply an explanation, for there was none to give. He had just taken a walk, that was all. But every time he was hesitant about answering why he had taken the walk, for fear of walking into a trap, Fallon would turn to the jury and raise his eyebrows. It is axiomatic that a sharp lawyer can make an innocent witness appear to drip with guilt. And that was exactly what Fallon did to the man who had gone out for a quart of milk but, once on the street, decided to take a little walk before returning home.

When he summed up to the jury, Fallon ignored practically everything except the walk of the milk purchaser. The jury decided that the milk purchaser had been hiding something—something he had done during that walk—and that if he was the kind of a character witness the defense produced the defendant must be guilty. So guilty he was.

In preparing a case against a defendant, Fallon had an unerring instinct for digging up something in the man's past which, sprung in the courtroom, usually threw a third strike at the defendant. Once he was trying a middle-aged man for stealing from his employer. The defendant had a good lawyer—a lawyer who put the defendant on the stand and established the fact that the man had led an honorable life from the cradle to the time he was accused of stealing. Everybody in the courtroom, including Fallon, knew that the defendant was making an excellent impression on the jury—an impression that cast serious doubt on the charge against him.

Now Fallon, taking over, asked the defendant if it weren't true that he had graduated from high school twenty-three years before.

"Yes, sir."

"And you had trouble in making a passing grade in history during your senior year in that high school. Isn't that correct?"

"Yes, sir." The defendant, who had been calm up to now, began to look a little uneasy.

"And you were accused of cheating in your final examination in history. Isn't that true?"

"No, not exactly."

"What do you mean not exactly?"

"Well, sir, several students in the senior class did a little copying from each other in history. But . . ."

"And you were one of those accused. Isn't that correct?"

"Well, you see . . ."

"Were you accused of cheating or weren't you!"

"I was. But . . ."

"Oh, so you *were* accused of cheating. That's all."

The man was sent up.

Fallon and Gene McGee used to go together to baseball games at the Polo Grounds. It was McGee who was a friend of John J. McGraw, the Giant manager, and it was McGee who introduced Fallon to the Little Napoleon. As Fallon and Mc-

Gee would sit in a box between home plate and first base, near the Giants' dugout, McGee would ask Fallon why he didn't quit Westchester County and come down to the big town and go into partnership with him. The pair, McGee pointed out, would make an unbeatable team. Fallon wasn't interested. His life, he said, was dedicated to meting out justice to evildoers. "It's how my mother wants it," he said to McGee more than once.

One day in 1915, after Fallon had been prosecuting for more than a year, he was trying a youth charged with a run-of-the-mill robbery. The defendant was a clean-cut, innocent-looking kid and the case against him was far from open and shut. There was some question in the district attorney's office, in fact, that the kid in the toils was guilty of the robbery. That, and the fact that the defendant had a clean record, was why the case was far from open and shut. But when Fallon laid hands on it, he proceeded to button it up. What he actually did, from all available accounts, was to blow up a fine circumstantial case against the youth and knock down everything in the defendant's favor introduced by a third-rate lawyer who was no match for him. So the kid went to prison. While the youth was in the big house his mother died of a stroke brought on, the doctor said, by emotional turmoil over her son's plight.

And then, a year later, another robber—an old pro—was caught in Westchester County. He began to sing, hoping to lessen his sentence. He included in his song a verse about the robbery that the kid had been sent up for a year before. The old pro had pulled that job, too.

Fallon, thinking the singing man was off key about the robbery he had sent the kid up for, questioned the singer in great detail. "How do I know you're not lying about that robbery?" Fallon asked the prisoner. "I can tell you the details about the house you say the kid broke into," said the old fellow. "All right," said Fallon, "go ahead and tell me." The old one described the interior of the house in great detail. Fallon was still not satisfied. "Well, will *this* satisfy you?" asked the prisoner. "I knocked over a piece of bric-a-brac and broke it when I pulled that job. I didn't see nothing about that in the papers."

Fallon now realized the criminal was speaking the truth. A piece of bric-a-brac *had* been broken during the robbery but never been mentioned in the press or during the trial of the boy in prison.

Fallon left his office early that afternoon. He walked into a saloon near the railroad station in White Plains—a saloon on the ground floor of a little broken-down hotel run by a couple of midgets who had once been performers in the Ringling Brothers-Barnum & Bailey Circus. The midgets were a husband-and-wife team and the husband, who stood about forty inches high and who went under the name of Admiral Dot, was the bartender. He had a special platform built behind the bar so that he could reach the beer spigots and the liquor bottles.

"Well, Bill," the Admiral said to Fallon that afternoon, "what'll it be—the usual?" "No," said Fallon, "give me a drink of whisky." The Admiral blinked. He had long served Fallon ginger ale and thought the fellow was kidding. But as he studied Fallon's face, he saw differently, and reached for a bottle.

Fallon later said that the first drink was hard to get down. But once he got it down he began to feel that creeping joy that overtakes thirsty wayfarers once they reach the oasis. The second drink was easy—and the third one was easier yet. Admiral Dot, who was a handy man with a bottle himself and therefore something of a connoisseur of drinkers of heroic stature, began to look upon Bill Fallon in a new and admiring light. "Bill," said the Admiral, "I must say you're off to a pretty good start for a fellow who's never touched the stuff."

Then Fallon told Admiral Dot that he had sent an innocent man to prison and that he had killed the prisoner's mother. "You're kiddin', Bill," said the Admiral. Fallon convinced the Admiral, and everybody else to whom the Admiral relayed the story, that he wasn't kidding. He chucked his job as assistant D. A. He was going to New York to practice law—criminal law—and give the Blind Goddess one of the worst beatings she was ever to get. Before he left, he saw that the innocent kid was pardoned.

The firm of Fallon and McGee began to operate out of a desk-and-hat-rack office in the Singer Building on lower Broadway. The word had soon seeped down from Westchester County, to the ears of the sharpies, that Bill Fallon was a smart mouthpiece who was out to beat the law. There was plenty of business for a fellow like that.

One of Fallon and McGee's first clients was a handsome big fellow in his middle thirties by the name of Robert Arthur Tourbillon, better known as Dapper Don Collins. Dapper Don had a vast repertoire of dodges for extracting money from people, his specialties being blackmail, card sharping on trans-atlantic liners, and confidence work.

It was Fallon who first asked Dapper Don how he had ever come to get into a career of taking the suckers. The answer was really quite simple. As a youth of eighteen in his native Georgia, young Tourbillon, seeking adventure, had latched into a job as a trick bicycle rider with a broken-down one-ring circus. Tour-billon, his manly frame set off in tights and spangles, rode a bicycle in a groove around the top of a roofless cage filled with lions. The lions appeared to be particularly nasty as they growled and leaped upward, trying to get at the handsome young cyclist. The peasants, who had paid their money to witness the death-defying spectacle, stood around the cage, awe-stricken and gawking, impressed by the belief that if the daring Tourbillon should make a slip and fall into the cage he would be torn to pieces.

Tourbillon laughed to himself as he rode around the rim of the cage and occasionally glanced at the yokels. While the lions looked particularly vicious actually they were completely harmless. They were all practically coming apart at the seams with age, and their teeth had been drawn and their claws clipped. It was while studying the spectators as he rode around the rim of the cage that the fellow who was later to become Dapper Don, con man *de luxe*, embraced the unshakable conviction that at least 25 per cent of the population were boobs ripe for the kill. And so he went on from there, cutting a high, wide, and hilarious swath through Larceny Lane.

The trouble for which Dapper Don Collins engaged the services of Fallon and McGee was quite pedestrian, really. Dapper Don had taken a well-known Bronx delicatessen dealer for about twenty thousand dollars in a crooked card game. Fallon, who instinctively liked the dapper one, asked Don if he had any of the money left—to put down as a retainer fee. "No, I haven't," said Collins. "But I expect to go over to New Jersey this coming weekend and I ought to have plenty Monday morning."

The situation was a ticklish one for Collins, even though the delicatessen dealer didn't have evidence for criminal prosecution. The mark swung a lot of weight with the Democratic political machine in the Bronx and he had told Collins to get up the money he had taken from him or he would apply political pressure to Dapper Don and see that he was run out of town.

"Have twenty thousand dollars here Monday if you can,

Don," said Fallon. "I'll be thinking of what to do over the week-end."

Fallon telephoned to a private detective and asked the dick to give him a quick rundown on the private life of the delicatessen dealer. On the Monday morning, when Dapper Don appeared with the twenty thousand dollars, Fallon counted it and put it in his pocket. "I'll just take this as my fee, Don," said Fallon. That was all right with Don, an easy-come-easy-go character, but he wanted to know what went with the delicatessen dealer.

It seemed that Fallon had run into a stroke of great fortune. The private dick he had put on the case had smelled out Bronx gossip to the effect that the big pastrami man, who had a wife and four children, also had a few mistresses around the Bronx, one of whom had given birth to a little bundle of joy. Don beamed. "You mean . . . ?" Fallon smiled and nodded. "The kid's a two-year-old boy and he looks exactly like that delicatessen man."

"But how sure are you, Bill?"

"I'll know tomorrow." The delicatessen man was coming into Fallon's office to talk about the Collins matter.

When, next day, the complainant appeared, he was the picture of upright belligerence. "I suppose," he told Fallon, "that you have sent for me so that you can settle up that crooked card game I was in."

"Well," said Fallon, "yes and no."

"Yes and no. What the hell do you mean!"

"How many children do you have?"

"Two boys and two girls."

"I mean *illegitimate* children. How many little bastards do you have besides that two-year-old boy on East 116th Street?"

The man said he didn't know what Fallon meant. But Fallon knew he had him. Fallon reached into a folder (as he later explained the dodge to drinking companions) and, holding the folder below the level of his desk top, out of range of the delicatessen man's vision, began to look at sheets of blank paper, one at a time. He would look at a sheet of blank paper, purse his lips, then make a ticking sound with his tongue and look up at the man sitting across the desk from him. Then he would shuffle the papers, look at another blank piece, and do the same thing. By the time he had pulled that a few times the delicatessen man was sweating. "My wife and family, Mr. Fallon!" he said. "You've got to think of *them.*"

Fallon told him he didn't have to worry about a thing. "Just forget about going to your political friends about Mr. Collins," he told the man, "and everything will be all right." Fallon put the blank papers back in the folder and put the folder in the safe. "Just what have you *got* in that folder, Mr. Fallon?" asked the man. "Never mind," said Fallon. "It'll never go any further so long as you keep your big mouth shut." That wrapped it up.

It was through Dapper Don Collins that Fallon met Arnold Rothstein, the big-time gambler who was later knocked off in the Park Central Hotel for welching on a big bet. Fallon, Collins, and Rothstein used to hang around the Astor Hotel and Times Square and, just for fun, play a little game with both the yokels and native New Yorkers, who are supposed to be very smart. They would bet with strangers that they could guess what make of automobiles would pass the hotel in preponderant numbers—five Fords before two Buicks, and so on, in a given period of time. They always won simply by "sticking" some automobiles around the corner and, after the bets were down, giving the signal to the drivers of the cars to infiltrate them into the Times Square traffic.

Another game that Fallon, Collins, and Rothstein played was to approach a stranger and say that they would give him odds that a friend of theirs—a fellow with a remarkable X-ray mind —could identify a given playing card simply by being called on the phone and asked what the card was. The feat sounded impossible but, after the bet was down, it always worked. The sucker would pick a card out of Rothstein's deck—the five of clubs, say—call a number, ask for a certain party, and ask him what card he was holding in his hand. The man with the X-ray mind would think a few seconds, then say, "Why, the five of clubs, of course."

The secret, since widely used, simply revolved around a code. Rothstein and the man on the other end of the phone had a file of fifty-two names, each representing one of the fifty-two cards in the deck. Thus if the sucker called the number and asked for Mr. Brown, the name Brown would indicate that he had picked the ace of spades, say. If he asked for Mr. Smith, that would indicate he had picked the two of spades. And so on. It was foolproof and, when they were short of lunch money, Fallon and McGee would pull the dodge, Fallon hanging around the Astor and McGee sitting in his office, with the code at his elbow and waiting for the phone to ring.

Fallon was hired to defend a little confidence man named Petey the Kid, who had sold Grant's Tomb to a sucker. The law had Petey the Kid bang to rights, as the saying went—identification of Petey by the sucker, witnesses to the swindle, and everything. The case was a real toughie but Fallon took it because Petey the Kid was in a position to plunk down around ten thousand dollars.

The district attorney was Ferdinand Pecora, later a state supreme court justice. Pecora, who felt his stomach muscles tightening every time he so much as heard Fallon's name, assigned one of his best assistants to prosecute Petey.

By way of revealing to the jury what a bad character the Kid was, Pecora's assistant reached into the records of Petey's past. Every time the prosecutor would bring out the pertinent data on something Petey had been mixed up in, Fallon would yowl an objection. He was overruled every time. "But what has this got to do with the issue at hand, Your Honor?" Fallon would ask the judge. "The evidence is admissible," the court would reply. Fallon would fold his arms and stare at the judge.

When it came time for Fallon to put his client on the stand, he knew that his only out was to play the case for laughs. "Petey," he asked, "are you acquainted with King George of England?" The prosecutor howled an objection. "The question is as pertinent as those asked by the State of New York," Fallon maintained. "Objection sustained," said the court.

"Petey," Fallon next asked, "were you—" and now he consulted some notes—"were you, on the night of February 12th last, a guest of President Wilson in the White House?" The prosecutor screamed and the judge almost broke his gavel and the jury began to laugh. Fallon insisted that the prosecutor had asked witnesses questions far less relevant. "Petey," Fallon next inquired, "have you ever climbed the large pyramid—the pyramid of Cheops?" Petey said he hadn't. "One of the two smaller ones, then?" No.

"Petey," said Fallon, consulting more notes, "an elderly couple were murdered in Pennsylvania, near Lancaster, several days before you were taken into custody. Do you deny that you murdered them?" Petey denied that he was a murderer. The jury was still laughing. "Petey," asked Fallon, "did you ever throw a baby out of a second-story window?" Petey hadn't. "Did you ever kick your mother downstairs?" Petey hadn't.

The jurors were practically laughed out when it came time for Fallon to sum up. "Take a look at this little man, gentlemen," he advised the jurors. "He has never thrown a baby out of a second-story window and he has never kicked his mother downstairs. And he has never climbed any of the pyramids." The jurors apparently spent their remaining laughter in the jury room because they brought in a split verdict.

Before Petey the Kid went on trial the second time, Fallon thought up a way of hanging another jury. His tack this time would be to concentrate on one juror, to the exclusion of other members of the panel. To do that he would have to find some common bond with the man.

A great one for improvising as he went along, Fallon had no idea of how he was going to establish a common bond with any of the jurors until, when questioning prospective members of the panel, he noticed that one man had difficulty walking. Obviously the man had rheumatism. Fallon accepted him without a question but with a comment: "May I say that I like your face?"

Next day Fallon appeared with a pained expression on his face. He didn't seem as spry as usual; in fact, he had difficulty moving around. The judge asked him if anything was wrong. "Nothing," said Fallon bravely. "Nothing at all, Your Honor, thank you."

"But there *is* something wrong with you, Mr. Fallon. You seem to be in pain."

"I'm afraid Your Honor has caught counsel in a falsehood," said Fallon. "I am indeed in great pain."

"What from, Mr. Fallon?"

"Rheumatism, Your Honor."

Eleven of the jurors voted to convict Petey the Kid but the rheumatic juror hung the panel. Thereafter the case of Petey the Kid was kicked around until it got lost.

Fallon was defending a big-time thief down in the Criminal Courts Building one day when the prosecutor appeared with a spanking new briefcase. The briefcase was filled with enough stuff to send Fallon's client up for a couple of hundred years. During the noon recess the prosecutor took the briefcase out to lunch with him. While at lunch, he got a telephone call. He got up from the table to go to the phone, taking the briefcase with him. There was a woman's voice on the other end of the wire. She inquired of the prosecutor if he were aware of the fact that his wife was unfaithful to him. The prosecutor was aware of no such thing but the inquiry startled him. It startled him so much that he forgot all about his briefcase, lying on the floor beside him. When the conversation was over, the briefcase was gone.

When the afternoon court session began, Fallon appeared, immersed in papers, and bathed in innocence. The prosecutor didn't show up. Fallon demanded to know where the man was. The judge explained that the session would have to be adjourned because the prosecutor had lost his briefcase. Fallon seemed shocked. But he quickly recovered from his shock. He demanded that the trial proceed. The judge overruled him. Finally the proceedings were adjourned until next morning while the prosecutor combed lower Manhattan for his briefcase.

Next morning the prosecutor still didn't have his briefcase. He had to admit that all his evidence had vanished. Fallon demanded that the trial proceed. It did. Fallon's client was, naturally, acquitted.

Bill Fallon was a whiz at taking a case that most other lawyers would have considered hopeless and, by a combination of artifices, pulling it out of the fire—always providing, of course, that the fee was right. Flossie Brooks, a shapely miss known on both sides of the law as a blackmailer *de luxe*, walked into the office of Fallon and McGee one day and announced that she was up to her pretty blue eyes in trouble.

"What have you done, Flossie?" asked Fallon, who knew the girl by reputation. Flossie had shaken down an Armenian rug merchant for a couple of thousand dollars and got caught at it.

"How did you get caught?" asked Fallon, looking at Flossie's legs. Flossie had learned that the Armenian, who was married and who lived in Manhattan, had done considerable nocturnal romping in Atlantic City while at the shore resort displaying rugs at a stand on the Boardwalk. In possession of this dreadful information, Flossie telephoned to the rug merchant's home. His wife answered the phone. "Let me speak to your husband," said Flossie. "Who is this?" asked the wife. "Never mind who it is," said Flossie. "Just let me speak to him."

Flossie got right to the point with the rug merchant. She thought maybe it would be worth a couple of thousand to the man if his wife didn't find out about what had happened at Atlantic City. "Sure," said the Armenian. "I'll be glad to attend to that matter. Where will I meet you?" A rendezvous was arranged for a spot in Central Park the following night.

The rug man began to think things over. He had heard somewhere that trying to buy off a blackmailer was like trying to get hold of a will-o-the-wisp. Then, too, his wife seemed curious about the call from the lady after business hours. He decided that confessing everything to his wife would entail less trouble in the long run than holding still for blackmail. So he confessed everything, took his beating, called the cops and appeared in Central Park next night with a couple of thousand in marked bills and two dicks hiding in the bushes.

"So when I took the money," Flossie told Fallon, "they pinched me."

When Flossie Brooks disclosed that she was in a position to

plunk down a handsome fee in advance, Fallon began to see the vague outlines of an acquittal. When the trial began, Fallon, keeping Flossie's legs in mind, told her to make sure she kept them crossed while he examined the talesmen. As he questioned each prospective juror as to his political affiliations, his religion, and other subjects having nothing whatever to do with the subject at hand, he didn't listen to any of the replies but studied the quizee to see how much attention he was paying to Flossie's legs. If the prospective juror seemed to be paying more attention to Flossie's legs than to Fallon, Fallon accepted him. His theory was that a man interested in a pretty pair of legs would, other things being equal, hardly be constrained to cast a vote to put them out of circulation.

The principal witnesses against Flossie were the Armenian rug merchant, his wife, and the two detectives who had grabbed Flossie after the rug man had given her the two grand in Central Park.

"You admit," asked Fallon when he began cross-examination of the rug merchant, "that the basis of this whole case against Miss Brooks arises from the fact that you were unfaithful to your wife on numerous occasions in Atlantic City?" "Yes," said the witness. "In other words," said Fallon, "you deceived your wife while you were in Atlantic City. Is that correct?" "Yes." "Or, to put it another way, you lied to your wife about what you did at night in Atlantic City." "Yes."

Fallon stepped closer to the rug man, who was squirming now, folded his arms across his chest, and looked at the witness with contempt. "My dear man," he said, "since you are a confessed liar, how do you expect these twelve fine gentlemen in the jury box here to believe you *now?*" Fallon, his arms still folded across his chest, turned to the jury and raised his eyebrows. "That is all," he said, still looking at the jury.

Then Fallon began to cross-examine the rug merchant's wife. He asked her if she were quite comfortable. Yes, she was. "Can I get you a drink of water or anything, Madam?" he inquired. No, she wasn't thirsty. "I think this courtroom is a little too warm," he said. "Shall I have a window opened for you?" No. The temperature was just right.

"Now, then, Madam," said Fallon, who seemed to put a low connotation on the word *madam*, "you have testified that you are positive that Miss Brooks here is the lady who telephoned to your husband the night of May 3rd last?" Yes, Madam was positive. "How many times have you heard Miss Brooks speaking?" Madam had heard Miss Brooks twice—the night she telephoned and after Miss Brooks was arrested.

"And you were certain, Madam, just from hearing the lady on the phone that night, that she was the same person that these two sterling detectives arrested in Central Park." The witness was positive. "In other words, Madam, if a stranger called your home on the telephone you could, just by hearing them speak two sentences, positively identify them later?" The witness gave an affirmative answer, but she didn't seem too sure of herself.

"Have you received any telephone calls lately from people you didn't know who asked to speak to your husband?" Madam had received several such calls.

"When did you receive the last such call?"

"Last night."

"What time?"

"Why, about half-past nine."

"And you would recognize the caller's voice if you heard it again?" The lady would. Fallon asked a man in the second row of spectators to stand up and come forward. He gave him a newspaper clipping to read. After the man had read for a minute or so, Fallon stopped him and asked the rug merchant's wife if she had ever heard the man before. "No," said the lady. "I've never heard the gentleman until just now."

Now Fallon put the man on the stand. He testified that he had, in the presence of witnesses, called the rug merchant's home the previous night.

"What time?"

"Half-past nine."

"Who answered?"

"A lady."

"Thank you, sir," said Fallon, who now turned to the jury, folded his arms, and raised his eyebrows. "That will be all," he said to the witness.

Fallon didn't have anything on the two detectives who had pinched his client but by the time he got through asking them questions that had nothing to do with the case some of the jurors were probably convinced that the kindest act either of the dicks had ever performed was to hold a lantern while his old mother went to a dark cellar to chop wood.

Everybody figured that Fallon was afraid to put his client on the stand. That was where Fallon fooled them. Flossie Brooks had a bad record and Fallon, taking the wind out of the prosecution's sails, brought out all the sordid details. Now he asked Flossie if she had a father and mother. Flossie did. "Do you support them?" Flossie had to. "Why?" "Well, my father has tuberculosis," said Flossie. "Oh," said Fallon, "I'm *so* sorry. And your mother?" Mother had a fatal heart ailment. Fallon looked as if he was about to break down and cry.

"Were you," Fallon now asked Flossie, "ever approached by any member of the New York Police Department and asked to pay tribute in lieu of being framed?" Flossie had been so approached. By whom? Why, by two detectives. "Do you see them in this courtroom?" Flossie pointed out the two prosecution witnesses. Fallon turned to the jury, folded his arms again and raised his eyebrows.

When the prosecutor began to cross-examine Flossie, Fallon kept shouting objections to practically every question. Finally the judge asked him to explain the basis of his objections. Fallon was glad the judge had raised the point. "Because, Your Honor," he said, "the prosecutor has political ambitions. He is not so much concerned about accepting the testimony of shaky and lying witnesses as he is to forward his political career."

The prosecutor began to scream. When the screaming stopped, Fallon asked the judge if he could make just one more statement. "I myself once had political ambitions," he said, "and, in my zeal, I sent an innocent man to prison. I have vowed to the memory of my dear mother that I shall do all in my power to see that no innocent man—or lady—ever goes to prison." Now Fallon turned on the actual tears. As he wiped them away, he apologized, in choking voice, to the judge and the twelve good men and true. It took the jury almost twenty minutes to bring in an acquittal for Flossie Brooks.

As time passed, Fallon became the darling of the newspaper boys. He was a man who was always good for some copy. There were always a couple of bottles of rye in the shabby little office of Fallon and McGee—one for Fallon and one for the scribes. By now Fallon was a fairly steady drinker—not a drunk by any means, but surely a man who could stand up to the rail with practically anybody. As a result he would often wake up in the morning with quite a head but, so far, he had never taken a hair of the dog that bit him before breakfast. It wasn't until later that he was to live on rye and raw eggs.

Fallon bought a house in the West Eighties—a four-story brownstone affair—and seemed devoted to his wife. He claimed that he always wanted children, particularly a son, but it was becoming increasingly apparent that his wish was not to be granted.

Now Fallon's mother died. When she died, something died inside him. He disappeared for a week—off on his first long bender.

The Broadway wise guys, such as Arnold Rothstein, the gambler, wondered how long it would be until Bill Fallon broke his marriage vows. The girls, particularly the type who hung around the Astor Hotel in Times Square, were, as Noel Coward might say, simply mad about the boy. Once in a while, he would go out on a party without his wife, but he always got home by midnight. His sole purpose in life seemed to be to hoodwink the law—by fair means if possible, by unfair means if need be.

Because so much of the business of Fallon and McGee—con men, con women, card sharps, and early-day racket boys—originated in the vicinity of Times Square, the firm, at Fallon's suggestion, left their downtown office and took one in Times Square. After a day in court, or in his office consulting with clients, Fallon would go into the Astor Hotel for dinner alone, then go out to see a show. He found that he got along fine with theatrical people. Some of them, such as David Belasco, used to attend his trials just to see him perform. He would return the compliment by going backstage after a performance and complimenting the actors.

Thus it was that Bill Fallon came to become an intimate friend of Fannie Brice. Fannie, a little East Side girl, had the emotional depth and the capacity for sympathy indigenous to the Jewish race. Though short on looks, with a large nose and a large mouth, when Fannie kneeled down on the stage of the New Amsterdam Theatre as a star of the Zeigfeld Follies and, bathed in a purple spotlight, sang a torch song, even the Broad-

way gamblers in the audience began to cry. Fallon, with his
Irish capacity for sentiment, thought Fannie Brice was one of
history's ten greatest women.

There was only one thing Fallon didn't like about Fannie
and that was her husband—Nicky Arnstein. Arnstein, who was
some fifteen years older than Fannie, was a fastidious gentleman, a highly sharpened product of a bitterly competitive society. He was a real hustler, mixed up in just about everything.
One of the best capsule descriptions of Arnstein was set down
by Gene Fowler in *The Great Mouthpiece*, the definitive
biography of William J. Fallon. "He," says Fowler of Arnstein,
"played a severe game of cards on transatlantic liners."

The Broadway wise guys—the Runyonesque characters who
are supposed to know everything—could never understand
why Fannie Brice, a very good girl, ever fell for a man like Arnstein. Fallon wondered, too. "Well, Bill, I'll tell you," Fannie
said to Fallon one night, "I just love the man. I guess I'll love
him till the day I die."

Fallon knew that Arnstein, in spite of his protestations to
Fannie that he was engaged in various legitimate enterprises,
would come a cropper sooner or later. When, then, one day in
February, 1920, some brokerage-house messengers were stuck
up in the Wall Street district and relieved of five million dollars
in negotiable securities, Fallon's underworld pipelines advised
him that Brother Arnstein had probably masterminded the little
plot.

Fallon dropped into the Arnstein apartment on Central Park
West. Arnstein was just having breakfast. Fannie, who had
worked in the Follies the night before, was still in bed. "Nicky,"
said Fallon, "a little bird tells me you know about that job down
on Wall Street." Arnstein went on with his breakfast. "You
don't have to tell me anything, Nicky," said Fallon. "But when

they catch up with you, let me know. I'll handle the case for Fannie's sake." Arnstein went on with his breakfast and Fallon left.

A couple of days later Fannie Brice telephoned to Fallon. "Nicky's gone, Bill," she said. "I'm afraid he's in some kind of trouble." Nicky was in big trouble. Some rat had peeped to the law and put the finger on Arnstein as the mastermind behind the big robbery. The New York district attorney, hearing that Fallon and Fannie Brice were close friends, and deducing that Fallon would be the lawyer in Arnstein's case, sent a couple of flatfeet to question Fallon as to where Arnstein was. "How should *I* know?" said Fallon. "But maybe if the district attorney agrees to a low bail for Arnstein I can find out where he is."

The D. A. wasn't in a mood to talk bail. Arnstein was a slippery customer and he wanted to put him practically in irons once he laid hands on him. So the D. A., figuring that Arnstein might be in touch with Fallon by long-distance phone, put taps on Fallon's office phone. Fallon was a little too cute for that. The dicks listening at the other end of the taps never heard Arnstein's voice. But Fallon, ever the joker, made certain that the eavesdropping of the dicks would be exciting. He had different friends phone him from public booths and say, "I just got a call from Nicky. He's leaving where he is and going where you told him to." The D. A.'s men, then the New York police, were run ragged trying to catch sight of the men who were calling Fallon with the exciting intelligence. But they never reached a phone booth in time to catch the callers.

Months passed. Arnstein was still lying doggo. Fallon kept in touch with the D. A. Finally the D. A. agreed to release Arnstein on a bail of $100,000 if Fallon produced him. "All right," said Fallon, "I'll bring Nicky in if you give me your word he won't be arrested on the way. This has to be a surrender, not a pinch. Nicky's a very sensitive fellow." It was a deal.

Fallon's partner, McGee, had been in touch with Arnstein all along—by long-distance phone and by letters Arnstein sent to intermediaries. Fallon met Arnstein one night at an inn in Mamaroneck. "I've arranged bail for you, Nicky," he said. "Who's putting it up?" asked Arnstein. "Arnold Rothstein." "Why, Rothstein hates me." "Yes, but he admires Fannie."

Fallon and Arnstein motored down from Mamaroneck to Manhattan next day in a new car Fallon had bought. The plot was to pick up Fannie Brice before Arnstein went down to Centre Street, surrendered to the D. A., and got out on bail. While on the way to pick up Fannie, Fallon and Nicky swung into Fifth Avenue and what did they do but run smack into the annual police parade. Arnstein was all for getting to hell off the avenue but Fallon thought it was a great joke. So there they were—the most wanted man in New York, and his mouthpiece —riding up Fifth Avenue with the cops.

Down on Centre Street, Arnstein went into the D. A.'s office alone to go through the formality of surrendering and getting out on bail. Fallon and Fannie left the car to go out and take a short walk. When they got back the car had been stolen. Fallon ducked into a phone booth and made a few calls. In a little while, a hairy gangster called Monk Eastman returned the car. "*Crise*, Bill," he said to Fallon, "how'd I know it was *your'n*."

Although Arnstein was quickly released on bail, there ensued a succession of developments that served as a springboard to make William J. Fallon a national figure. Arnstein was ordered to appear before a United States commissioner and answer some questions relating to his financial standing. Fallon knew that if Arnstein answered the questions truthfully he would hang himself and that if he lied he could be indicted for perjury.

Fallon, who could soak up information like a sponge when he had to, sat up all night reading the federal statutes that might be of help to him in getting his client out of the jam. He thus became intrigued by the possibilities inherent in the constitutional amendment that holds that a man may refuse to testify on the grounds that his own testimony may degrade and incriminate him.

So, when Arnstein appeared before the United States commissioner to answer questions, he began to answer, then suddenly clammed up on the grounds that he might degrade and incriminate himself. Nicky's fear of degrading himself seemed somewhat academic but he was on solid ground in fearing to incriminate himself. The commissioner blinked when he heard Arnstein parroting the words that Fallon had obviously put in his mouth, then looked at Fallon. There stood Fallon, with his arms folded across his chest. "I suppose," the commissioner said to Fallon, "that your client is acting on your instructions." "He certainly is," said Fallon.

The commissioner, not exactly a pushover, had heard the refusal-to-answer-on-constitutional-grounds dodge before and so had other judges. But up until now the men on the bench had brushed the dodge by simply saying, in effect, "You'll answer or go to jail," and the defendants had usually answered. But this time it was to be different. Nicky refused to answer and the commissioner ordered him to jail.

Fallon dived into the statutes again. While Arnstein sweated it out in durance vile, Fallon whipped up an application for *habeas corpus*. But no judge would sign the application. "Don't worry about a thing," Fallon told Arnstein. "I'm going to take this whole matter direct to the United States Supreme Court."

By a series of intricate legal maneuvers, Fallon quickly got his *habeas corpus* proceedings in the calendar of the highest court in the land. And so Mr. Fallon went to Washington.

As a rule, attorneys suffer from stage fright when making a maiden appearance before the austere justices. But not Fallon. He strutted like a peacock when he made his appearance before the Nine Old Men as he argued that his client should be legally sprung.

Most lawyers appearing before the august tribunal wore formal morning attire. Fallon wore his usual blue serge suit and burgundy necktie. Veteran reporters, witnessing his appearance, thought they detected an unusual stiffness in some members of the bench.

Fallon was obviously steeped in the statutes relating to *habeas corpus,* thoroughly grounded, however recently. As he spoke, his tone was just the right combination of confidence and respect. He hadn't been at his argument long when the colder justices seemed to start thawing out. Although Fallon was talking about dry legal technicalities he might as well have been telling a smoking-car story for the interest he created.

Once in a while, a justice would interrupt him to ask him a question. During one such interrogation, Fallon forgot himself and folded his arms across his chest—something that was and is unthinkable in the Supreme Court chambers. But he quickly remembered where he was and dropped his arms to his sides. When it was all over, he bowed, like somebody in a palace in Versailles in the eighteenth century, and left the chambers. Outside, he inquired of a lawyer acquaintance, "Where can I get a drink?"

The Supreme Court quickly handed down its decision—in favor of Fallon. Legally sprung, all Arnstein had to worry about now was going to jail again—on the bond robbery charge.

It was while in Washington that Fallon met the great love of his life. He went alone to Keith's Theatre one night to see a vaudeville show. One of the acts featured a young dancer named Gertrude Vanderbilt—no relation to *the* Vanderbilts since she had red, rather than blue, blood. Miss Vanderbilt, a divorcee, was in her twenties, some ten years younger than Fallon.

Fallon became so entranced with the girl that he went around to the stage door afterward and sent in his card. Gertrude Vanderbilt had heard all about Fallon, both in New York and in Washington.

"I've fallen in love with you," Fallon said to Miss Vanderbilt as he talked to her in her dressing room. Gertrude thought he must be kidding. "No," said Fallon, "I'm serious. I've never been so serious. You're what I've been looking for all my life." Gertrude leaned forward and smelled Fallon's breath. "I thought so," she said. "You've been drinking." "I had only a few before I came to the show," Fallon said. "Well, all I can say is they were pretty powerful."

By this time, Fallon was used to having his way with women. He began to pout. "You are," said Gertrude Vanderbilt, showing him to the door of the dressing room, "the most conceited man I've ever met in my whole life. I'd be much obliged if I never laid eyes on you again."

Fallon went back to New York talking to himself. Back in the big town, he began to strut. He also began to play the field. But he told Gene McGee that he couldn't get the Vanderbilt girl out of his mind. He said he would have liked to marry her but that naturally his religion forbade divorce. McGee, who knew of Fallon's almost unnatural attachment for his dead mother, asked him if the dancer in any way resembled his mother. "That's the odd part of it," said Fallon. "Not the slightest."

The bond robbery case involving Arnstein took an unexpected turn. The federal authorities decided that they had a better chance of going to bat against Arnstein in Washington than in New York. It turned out that Arnstein had been seen in the nation's capital in company with several men known to have disposed of some of the stolen bonds through a fence there. He had been registered at a hotel under an assumed name and a porter on a New York-Washington train had served him in a drawing room the night before he had registered at the hotel. The case against Arnstein was, in fact, circumstantial, but dangerous to the man, principally because of his unsavory reputation.

At Arnstein's trial, Fallon pulled out the usual stops—confusing the government's witnesses and making them contradict themselves and causing them to create unfavorable impressions on the jurors. Fallon gave the colored porter quite a rough ride on the witness stand. He felt on pretty sure ground there for some of the jurors, he knew, had southern, anti-Negro sentiments. Result: a hung jury.

Fallon was still carrying the torch for Gertie Vanderbilt. Arnstein, an unreasonable character, blamed Fallon's interest in the dancer for the jury disagreeing rather than acquitting him. He started to call Gertie foul names. Fallon told him to take back what he said. Arnstein wouldn't do it. "All right," said Fallon, "you can get another lawyer to handle your next trial."

Arnstein ate crow. He pleaded with Fallon to keep the case. Fallon gave him a withering look and left for New York. He disappeared. Fannie Brice tried to find him and make him reconsider her husband's case. Fallon paid no attention.

One night Fallon went to a performance of the Zeigfeld Follies. He sat down front watching Fannie singing her greatest song, one that was written especially for her to express her feelings about Arnstein—*My Man*. Fallon was moved—but not moved enough to go to bat for Arnstein. Arnstein had said something nasty about the girl Fallon loved and, despite the fact that he had not, as yet, reached first base with Gertrude Vanderbilt, he was completely off his head about the girl.

Eugene McGee handled Arnstein's second trial in Washington. Arnstein was convicted of complicity in the bond robbery and given a jolt in the federal penitentiary.

Arnstein's conviction sent Fallon's stock up. The Broadway wise guys—the characters that Damon Runyon, then a young reporter, was already studying—were more than ever convinced that Bill Fallon was unbeatable.

Eventually, Fallon and Gertie Vanderbilt came to terms. He bought her a handsome house on the upper West Side. If the man was in love with her she was, by now, completely in love with him. The Fallon-Vanderbilt love affair became, in fact, the eighth wonder of the world to Broadway, which didn't know what the other seven wonders were. The pair were always seen around town when Gertie was playing in or near New York. When she was on the road, Fallon was on the road, too, leaving McGee to take care of the firm's business. Mrs. Fallon of course knew about Miss Vanderbilt but she always hoped the affair would run its course.

Fallon was a great believer in the benefits of delaying a trial. There were several reasons for such a belief. Witnesses died, or their memories grew dim or blacked out all together. Evidence deteriorated or, more happily, vanished. The winds of public sentiment shifted.

Fallon had one case dumped in his lap which he immediately

set about delaying because public sentiment was so unfavorable to his client. The client was a taxi driver named Schmidt. He owned his own cab and, after driving fares around town, picked up women on his own time. One night in a ruckus in the back seat of his cab he injured a woman internally and she bled to death.

Schmidt was held without bail on a charge of murder. The papers wanted Schmidt's scalp and Schmidt screamed for Fallon.

Fallon, learning that Schmidt was well heeled, took the case. He pulled every trick out of the bag to put as much time as possible between the girl's death and the beginning of Schmidt's trial. He would have to appear in another court somewhere on a prior matter. He would have to be out of town on legal business.

Then, too, Fallon would fake illness. Some broken-down doctor would appear in court for him, on the eve of Schmidt's trial, and convince the judge that counsel was practically at death's door. Once Fallon appeared himself to ask for a postponement because of illness. McGee and another man held him up as he appeared before the bar and, in a loud whisper, requested the delay. Court attendants, though used to Fallon's trickery, were afraid the man was in such bad shape that he might not leave the courtroom alive.

A whole year passed. During that time the fires of public resentment against Schmidt lessened in intensity. But Schmidt signed three separate confessions to the murder. The confessions didn't worry Fallon. He would find a way to get around them.

For several days before the trial began, Fallon boned up on medical books. Thus he went into court knowing practically as much about the physical peculiarities of the female body as the average doctor—more, in fact, than some medicos.

The state, which had its innings first, produced enough doctors to staff a small hospital to prove the death was murder. By way of conditioning the jury to the line he was to take, Fallon, in cross-examining the state's doctors, continually referred to the girl's death as "this accident." The prosecutor, growing tired of that, began to bellow objections. This was no accident, it was murder. The more the prosecutor objected, the more Fallon referred to "this accident."

When the state's case was in, Fallon pulled his first big surprise. He summoned as a defense witness Dr. Otto H. Schultz, a medical examiner who had helped prepare the case *against* Schmidt. The prosecution objected to the move on a technicality. The prosecution lost.

Fallon played cat-and-mouse with Dr. Schultz. Finally he got Dr. Schultz to admit that the death of the woman could have been accidental.

Next Fallon called on the woman's husband—from whom she had been separated at the time of her death. He inquired of the husband if it were true that his wife had frequently suffered internal hemorrhages. Yes, it was true. "Then you don't believe what the police say," said Fallon, "that your wife died because of any guilty act on the part of the defendant?" No, the husband did not believe such a thing.

Next morning, when court opened, something new had been added—the taxicab in which the death had occurred. The taxicab was as essential to the case as a fifth wheel is to wagon. But it produced a very dramatic effect.

Now Fallon summoned Schmidt to the stand in his own defense. "Now I want you to tell the truth—the whole truth, Mr. Schmidt," said Fallon. "I want you to hold nothing back from these gentlemen of the jury. You are married?" Yes, Schmidt was married. "Then you were unfaithful to your wife in consorting with other women?" Yes, Schmidt had been unfaithful. "Did you love your wife?" Yes, Schmidt had loved his wife. "Did you love any of the other women you consorted with?" No—except one.

"Which one, Mr. Schmidt?" Schmidt had loved the lady he was accused of killing. "You didn't love any of the other women, but you loved the woman you are accused of killing?" "Yes, Mr. Fallon." "Did you kill your wife, Mr. Schmidt?" "No." "Why?" "Well, I love her." "Did you kill the lady who had this *accident*, Mr. Schmidt?" "Why, no. She just bled to death."

Fallon turned to look at the taxicab. "This is the cab where the accident occurred?" That was the cab. Fallon opened the front door of the cab. "You were here in this front seat with the lady, Mr. Schmidt?" No, Schmidt had been in the back seat. Fallon opened the rear door and peered in. "In *here?*" Yes, in there.

"Who suggested that the two of you go into the back seat?" "I object," yelled the prosecutor. The objection was overruled. Fallon smiled sadly. "I am certain, Mr. Prosecutor," he said, more in sorrow than anger, "that my client is not going to give the answer you feared he would give." Now to Schmidt: "As I was asking, before we were interrupted, who suggested that you and the lady leave the front seat of your cab and go into the back seat?" "I did," said Schmidt. "You are a very honest man, Mr. Schmidt. And now, may I ask, did the lady object in any way, either by word or action, to your suggestion that the two of you go into the back seat?" "No, she didn't." "Are you sure of that—dead sure she didn't object?" "Yes. Matter of fact, she said she wanted to go to the back seat." Fallon turned to look at the jury and slightly raised his eyebrows.

"Mr. Schmidt, I notice that your right arm seems to pain you. Is something wrong with it?"

"Yes, sir. It was twisted."

"Twisted? By whom?"

"By the people who got the confessions from me."

"Mr. Schmidt, you have made three confessions. Which one resulted in your twisted arm?"

"My arms were twisted *twice*."

Fallon appeared shocked. "Twice! Then you were constantly mistreated by the police so you would sign those three confessions?"

"All the time."

"In other words, the confessions were forced out of you."

"Yes, sir."

The D. A. was up screaming an objection. "Objection sustained," said the judge. "Why, Your Honor?" asked Fallon. "My client has marks all over his body." "Objection sustained." Fallon told Schmidt to pull up his pants legs. The legs were cut and otherwise marked up. The D. A. yelled that the marks had been there at the time of Schmidt's arrest. He objected and the objection was sustained. "What has happened to justice?" Fallon muttered so that only the jurors could hear him.

Fallon had completely knocked the wind out of state's sails before the prosecutor got to Schmidt. He had revealed the worst about Schmidt, then capitalized on it. Schmidt was acquitted.

Fallon was a great one for keeping an ear to the ground, the better to tune in on anything that he could twist to his financial advantage. He was talking to his friends, Jack Doyle, the Broadway betting commissioner, and John J. McGraw, manager of the Giants, a couple of nights before the 1919 World Series between the Chicago White Sox and the Cincinnati Reds was about to begin at Redland Field in Cincinnati.

"There's somethin' goddamned funny goin' on out there," McGraw said to Fallon. "Jack here'll tell you why." Doyle had become suspicious of all the money that had suddenly appeared in support of the Reds, who were very much the underdog in the series. The betting had originally started out 5-2 in favor of the White Sox, a superb baseball machine, and then, as the opener in the series drew near, Cincinnati partisans were offering even money that their club would take the autumn classic.

"Sounds like something has been fixed," said Fallon.

"You can bet your last dollar somethin's been fixed," growled McGraw.

The first game at Redland Field seemed to bear out McGraw's and Doyle's suspicions. Eddie Cicotte, the star pitcher of the White Sox, whose most puzzling delivery was the shine ball, didn't have his stuff; the Reds hit him almost at will. The White Sox sluggers—Shoeless Joe Jackson and a couple of others—didn't seem to be giving it the old college try. Sports writers noted that Jackson in particular seemed to be off balance at the plate. So the White Sox dropped the opener.

The series of 1919 went to the first club that took five games, not four. The Reds took the classic five games to three. The Sox looked like the champs they were in the three games they won. They looked incredibly bad in the five games they lost. It didn't add up.

Fallon saw McGraw when McGraw returned to New York from the series. "If any damned thing was ever fixed," McGraw said to Fallon, "that series out there was."

"Who'd you see that looked suspicious, John?" asked Fallon.

"Well, I saw Abe Attell hanging around the Stinton Hotel in Cincinnati lookin' like the cat that ate the bird."

Abe Attell rang a bell with Fallon. Attell, the onetime fly-weight boxing champion of the world, had quit the ring with a quarter of a million dollars but got rid of it fast. It had behooved him to turn a buck practically any way he could. So he had taken to turning quite a few bucks on sure-thing gambling.

The rumor that the World Series had been fixed—that Eddie Cicotte, Shoeless Joe Jackson, and several other White Sox players had taken a dive—gained momentum all winter long. It was still very much alive when the baseball season opened in April of 1920. All this while, Fallon was trying to figure a way of putting the big swindle on a paying basis.

Still keeping his ear very close to the ground, Fallon was eventually able to reconstruct just about what had happened. Some weeks before the series had opened, some gamblers had approached Arnold Rothstein, the big-time Broadway gambler, with a fine proposition. The White Sox looked like a shoo-in for the American League pennant and the Reds ditto for the National League flag. Although the White Sox were the great-est club in baseball, they were torn by internal strife. Many of the star players, including Eddie Cicotte, the star pitcher, were dissatisfied with the coolie wages they were getting. They were so dissatisfied, in fact, that they were sore. "So you see, A. R.," one gambler said to Rothstein, "the boys would listen to a prop-osition." The proposition that the gamblers had was that Roth-stein put up one hundred thousand dollars as an advance payoff for certain key White Sox players to throw the series, then everybody could get down on Cincinnati to take the series, at very attractive odds, and mop up.

Rothstein asked who had thought up the bright idea. "Abe Attell," said one of the boys. "I don't think I'll put up the money," said Rothstein. Rothstein was smart enough there. He knew that if Attell was behind the plot that he would somehow scrape up the hundred grand, or part of it, somewhere else. So why should *he* put up the money?

Rothstein's listening posts advised him that Attell and some of his pals had scraped up enough for the fix. So Rothstein, without actually underwriting the fix, plunged heavily at highly favorable odds.

Learning all this, Fallon now had his angle. He called on Rothstein. "Arnold," he said, "you're in trouble." How? "It's that World Series business." Rothstein said he had had nothing to do with it. "I know," said Fallon. "I know. But that's not what Charley Comiskey thinks." Charles Comiskey, known as the Old Roman, was the tough-minded, tough-talking owner of the White Sox. "Why," Rothstein asked Fallon, plainly scared, "what's Comiskey saying about me?"

"Don't worry about a thing," said Fallon. "But phone me if he starts getting tough."

Old Roman Comiskey came to New York when the White Sox came in to play their first 1920 series with the Yankees. Fallon phoned him at his hotel. "You don't know me," Fallon said to Comiskey, "and who I am doesn't matter. I just love the game of baseball and I thought you'd like to know something about that World Series last fall."

"Keep talking," said the Old Roman.

"You might call to see Arnold Rothstein. He's the man who fixed it."

Next day Fallon got a phone call from Rothstein. Rothstein was frantic. "Get up here right away," he told Fallon. "That man from Chicago is waiting outside my office."

Fallon burst in on Rothstein and Comiskey. "Who are you?" he demanded of the man he had telephoned the day before.

Comiskey identified himself. "Well, I'll have to ask you to get out of here." Comiskey said he hadn't a mind to leave. Fallon picked up a telephone. He called the precinct station house. "This is William J. Fallon speaking," he said. "I'm with Mr. Arnold Rothstein. I wish you would send an officer around here immediately to arrest a man for trespassing."

"Wait a minute!" shouted Comiskey, who probably figured he was in enough trouble. "I'll go." Fallon called off the cops and the Old Roman left with his toga tattered.

But the Old Roman was not through. He put private detectives on the trail. As a result several gamblers, associates of Attell in the fix, were picked up in Chicago. They sang. Attell, six White Sox players, and three other gamblers were indicted for conspiracy—then a serious charge in Chicago.

Fallon dropped in to see Rothstein. "Arnold," he said, "I'm afraid they'll indict you next. You better go out there and appear before the grand jury."

"Are you *crazy?*" said Rothstein.

"On the contrary, you'll be crazy if you don't go out there and demand that the grand jury hear you. Some of those other rats are trying to frame you." Of course nothing of the kind was happening, but after Comiskey's visit, Rothstein thought the roof was caving in. "What'll I *say* to the grand jury?" asked Rothstein. "Just tell them the whole truth. Say you were approached by men you didn't know and that you decided not to go into the thing because if it was going to be fixed you could clean up without incriminating yourself."

"*Say,*" said Rothstein, "I see what you mean."

"The truth, Arnold," said Fallon, "is always the best policy." And now, Fallon added, he was a little short. Could Rothstein advance him a little matter of ten thousand dollars or so? Rothstein was glad to oblige.

Rothstein made quite a hit in Chicago with the jurors. The man's honesty appealed to the jurors. So he returned to New York with a clean bill of health.

Now Fallon decided he could pick up some extra money from Abe Attell. He contacted Attell and cautioned the little man that he was in desperate need of good counsel. Attell agreed. "Fine," said Fallon. "I think I can square that matter out in Chicago for about fifteen thousand dollars."

Attell handed over the money and Fallon left town for a few days. During his absence, Attell was arrested by the New York authorities at the request of the Chicago authorities, to be held pending extradition to face the conspiracy indictment. Fallon, who had apparently been very busy while out of town, now returned and pulled one out of the hat. He went before a judge and, demanding that Attell be released, claimed that the Abe Attell who was arrested was not the same Abe Attell who had been indicted in Chicago.

"On what grounds do you base such an assertion?" asked the judge.

"Either there are two Abe Attells, Your Honor," said Fallon, "or somebody in Chicago *posed* as my client."

"What proof have you to back up your assertion?" asked the judge.

Fallon said he could produce a Chicago man who had gone before the grand jury in Chicago and contributed to the indictment of Abe Attell simply by identifying a picture of the man he said he had worked with to fix the series.

So Abe Attell was brought before the judge and Fallon produced the man who had testified before the Chicago grand jury. "No," said the Chicagoan, "that ain't the man I worked with on the series. That ain't him at all." So Abe Attell was never extradited to Chicago and the case against him collapsed of its own weight. The other conspirators got off, too, but the guilty players were banned for life from organized baseball and Judge K. M. Landis became baseball's first commissioner.

Precisely what went on between the time Fallon approached Abe Attell to become his counsel and the day Attell was pointed out by the Chicagoan as *not* the Abe Attell who had fixed the series has never come to light. But we can *guess*, can't we?

Fallon was perhaps the first of several smart New York lawyers who have pulled what some legal strategists call the smell trick in a courtroom. He was defending a fierce-looking big Russian who was accused of arson. The defendant had a record that was somewhat against him. He had been convicted twice previously of setting fire to furniture stores he had operated and attempting to collect insurance on the fires. And now here he was with his liberty on the line for his third try at the jackpot.

The whole case, by the time Fallon got through twisting it around, revolved around some rags that a fireman had come across in the burning building. A fireman got on the stand and testified that the rags had been soaking wet and that when he had smelled them he had smelled kerosene. Fallon just sat there, eyeing the fireman as the man testified.

When it came Fallon's time to cross-examine the witness, he approached the fireman in what seemed to some veteran courtroom attachés as a deceptively friendly manner. "You are, I suppose," Fallon began, "an expert on smells."

"Well," answered the fireman, "I kind of have to be. You got to look out for suspicious smells when you go out on a fire so's to make sure it ain't incendiary."

"I see," said Fallon. "And so when you went out to fight this particular blaze you were looking for suspicious smells. Is that correct?"

"Well, kind of."

"You knew, of course, that the defendant in this action had been convicted of arson twice before?"

"Yes, I knew that."

"You were aware of that fact when the bell rang in the fire-house and you found out where the fire was."

"No. Not when the bell rang, but when I got to the fire."

"At any rate, you were *suspicious* that this particular fire might have been of incendiary origin when you got to it to put it out?"

"Yes, sir."

"That being the case, you naturally looked around for some evidence to corroborate your suspicions."

"Naturally. Yes, sir."

"And so you picked up these rags which you say were soaked in this highly inflammable fluid."

"Yes, sir."

"You smelled the rags and decided they were soaked with kerosene?"

Right.

"I notice those rags were not introduced in evidence. Why is that, may I ask?"

"Well, I dropped them to go on fighting the fire and by the time I got back to where I found them they had been burned up."

"But you're sure you're not *lying* about those rags. You really found such rags when you first reached the blaze."

Of course the fireman was not lying.

"All right," said Fallon, "I'll take your word for it that you are telling the truth. You *look* like a truthful man. But now I want to ask you something else. Are you sure that that was kerosene—and not *water*—that you smelled on those rags?"

The fireman seemed puzzled that Fallon should ask him such

a question. Fallon repeated the question. Certainly the fireman was sure. He certainly knew the difference between water and kerosene when he smelled the two. "You're *absolutely* sure about that?" said Fallon. The fireman was absolutely sure.

"Then," said Fallon, "you would not object to *proving* to these fine gentlemen here"—Fallon pointed to the jurors—"that you can tell the difference between water and kerosene when you smell them." No, the fireman would not object; he was, in fact, slightly amused. "Do not take this matter lightly," said Fallon. "A man's liberty depends on whether you can tell the difference when you smell kerosene and water."

Fallon went back to counsel table and produced five bottles, each filled with liquid. The bottles were numbered 1, 2, 3, 4, and 5. He took the cork out of bottle No. 1 and handed the bottle to the witness. "Smell that," he said, "and tell me what's in it." The fireman took a smell. "Kerosene," he said. "Take a *good* smell," said Fallon. "I want you to be certain that you do not make a mistake." The fireman took a deep smell. "Kerosene," he repeated.

Now Fallon handed the witness bottle No. 2 and had him repeat the test. "Kerosene," said the fireman. The witness said that bottles 3, 4, and 5 also contained kerosene. When Fallon took bottle No. 5 from the fireman he put it to his lips and took a drink of it. Now he held the bottle to the nose of each juror. "Gentlemen," he said to the jurors, "the contents of this bottle do not taste like kerosene to me. And I am very sure they do not smell like kerosene to you." He paused to savor the drama of the situation. "And now I'll tell you why the contents of this bottle do not taste or smell like kerosene. This bottle—this bottle that the gentleman on the witness stand would have you believe contains kerosene—doesn't contain kerosene at all. It contains water. When you get into the jury room I wish you would all help yourselves to a taste of its contents. If what you taste in the slightest resembles kerosene I think it is your duty to convict my client. If what you taste is water, then it is your duty to acquit my client."

Of course the client was acquitted. What Fallon had done, simply, was to fill the fireman's smelling apparatus with kerosene fumes by having the man inhale deeply of the first four bottles. Then, when he whiffed the water, the kerosene fumes from the previous four bottles were still in his nostrils and he thought the water was kerosene.

The early Twenties in New York was the golden age for the Bucket Boys. They were the fellows who operated bucket shops, or crooked brokerage houses. There was no Securities and Exchange Commission to regulate brokerage houses in the Twenties and the way the boobs were taken by the sharpers was really something awful.

All a crooked outfit needed to make a quick quarter of a million or so was an office somewhere and a few telephones. A squad of sharpers would sit at the telephones, systematically go through the telephone directory and, in golden tones, call people all day long. They would pose as customer's men from a respectable brokerage and take orders for listed stocks at the market price. The gimmick was that they didn't buy the ordered stock, but just took the customer's money and held it in the hope that the stock would go down. Then they'd have a profit of the price difference instead of a lousy brokerage fee. If the stock went up, they'd talk the client into reinvesting in some other stock until that went down—for a while a very profitable enterprise.

Finally, however, the federal people began to bring down a few of the bucketeers and that's where Fallon got into the act.

He added to his repertoire the defense of about half the city's crooked brokers.

There were two ways to get a bucketeer off the federal hook: confusing the jury so that the least it would bring in would be a disagreement, or purchasing a juror. In the light of subsequent events, it would seem that Fallon purchased quite a few jurors. Newspaper reporters, not to say federal judges and prosecutors, began to take notice of the imposing number of eleven-to-one verdicts Fallon got when representing a bucketeer. The *New York American* made one reference to him as Eleven-to-One Fallon.

When, however, there was something less than an open-and-shut case against a bucketeer, Fallon tried for an acquittal. He had quite a bag of tricks in trying for acquittals. In one typical case, which rotated around a sucker identifying a bucketeer on the witness stand, Fallon simply had his client completely alter his appearance. He put the man on a severe diet and reduced him from two hundred pounds to one hundred forty. He changed the color of the defendant's hair from brown to black, mixed with gray. He had the man shave off a naturally imposing moustache and wear needless eyeglasses so thick that they looked like magnifying glasses. To top off everything, he sent the defendant to a dramatic coach and vested him with a southern accent.

After the sucker had testified for the government, Fallon cross-examined him at length about the appearance of the villain who had bilked him out of his life's savings. The sucker described the villain as a moustached, brown-haired man weighing about two hundred pounds who talked like a typical New Yorker. "And did he wear eyeglasses?" asked Fallon. "No." "You're *sure* about that?" Positively.

When Fallon put the defendant on the stand, the man got up

from the counsel table and began to walk toward the witness chair. He walked into the counsel table and fell over it. "Why," said Fallon, "you're so nervous you forgot to put on your glasses. There's nothing to be nervous about. The complainant in this case certainly wasn't talking about *you*."

So the villain put on the thick-lensed glasses and took the stand, and made a categorical denial of the charge against him in moss-and-honeysuckle tones. Then Fallon asked the sucker to stand up. "Is this the man you say took your money?" he asked the sucker, pointing to the defendant. "No," said the sucker.

Acquittal.

In the case of another bucketeer, Fallon brought his defendant into court on a stretcher with a doctor and nurse in attendance. The federal prosecutor protested that the defendant was faking. Fallon had half a dozen doctors testify on the stand that the crook had a few months to live—if he was lucky. The government prosecutor demanded that *his* doctors examine the defendant. The Fallon doctors, men who were hardly burdened by adherence to the Hippocratic oath, had dosed the man with drugs that had made his heart beat almost twice as fast as normal, and coached the crook in how to simulate symptoms of half a dozen fatal ailments. The government doctors had to admit that the defendant was at death's door. It took the jury almost ten minutes to acquit the man.

Fallon's eleven-to-one verdicts in the cases of bucketeers eventually aroused the suspicion of William Randolph Hearst's *New York American*. So the Hearst paper assigned a flock of reporters to shadow the jurors who had thrown the verdicts into disagreement. The boys dug up a man named Rendig who seemed to be unexplainably flush with money. Rendig had cast the sole dissenting vote when a jury wanted to convict two partners in a bucket shop who were represented by Fallon in federal court. The *American* reporters turned their dope over to the United States Attorney and Rendig confessed that Fallon had paid him five thousand dollars to hang the jury.

Thus it was that William J. Fallon went on trial in the summer of 1924 at the age of thirty-six. The trial was looked upon by a sweating populace as something of a circus. Gene McGee, Fallon's partner, was the counsel of record in the case but when things got under way, Fallon personally took over. He had been hitting the bottle hard for some weeks before the trial but Gertie Vanderbilt got him to lay off at least until the trial was over.

Fallon, dressed in a new blue suit and wearing a new burgundy necktie, was his old self in the courtroom—the actor responding to the stimulus of an appreciative audience. He cocked his head, folded his arms across his chest, and bowed from the waist as the judge spoke to him.

The crux of the whole case was, of course, the testimony of Rendig, the purchased juror. The money that had been paid to Rendig had reached him by way of two checks, which in turn had gone through half a dozen persons before Rendig endorsed them. Fallon made a great deal of that. Rendig's receipt of the checks had been part of a plot—a plot by William Randolph Hearst to ruin him. And why had Hearst tried to plot his ruin?

Fallon pulled another spectacular one out of the hat. He took the stand in his own defense. He began to question himself.

Hearst had tried to ruin him, Fallon said, because he had gone to Mexico and there dug up birth certificates of twins that Hearst had fathered through a certain motion-picture actress. The jurors sat there with their mouths open, inhaling the scandal.

The government's prosecutor screamed objections until he

practically wore himself out. The Mexican business, true or false, had nothing to do with the jury purchasing yet Fallon made it, rather than the issue at bar, the big thing. He made so much of it, in fact, that the jurors were thinking more about Hearst and the movie actress than about Fallon. One of Hearst's editors, shaken at the testimony, telephoned Hearst at the Hearst ranch in California and told him what Fallon had said. "Well," said Hearst, "you won't have to think twice about what your lead headline will be tomorrow."

Then, of a steaming midsummer morning, William J. Fallon got up to address the jury—to plead for his professional life. That was the day he made his great, tear-jerking summation on his own behalf—one of the most dramatic summations in American courtroom history. It wasn't altogether *what* Fallon said in his summation; much of the power was in *how* he said it—the tone of voice, the facial expressions, the dramatic gestures. Spectators who were in that courtroom that hot day almost a third of a century ago never, to their dying day, will forget the performance of the great mouthpiece pleading for his professional existence. And then, at the end of his summation, when Fallon stood there, with his head bowed and his arms at his side, a strange stillness enveloped the entire courtroom.

That night, after the prosecution had summed up to the jury and the judge had charged it, the jurors brought in their verdict. *Not guilty*. Fallon, sitting there waiting for the verdict, jumped to his feet, rushed over to the jury box, and shook the hand of each talesman. Then, on his way out of the jury room, he walked over to Nat Ferber, one of the *American* reporters who had helped build up the jury-bribing case against him. "Nat," Fallon whispered, "so help me God, *I'll never bribe another juror*."

Fallon went to the Polo Grounds next day to watch the game between the Giants and the Reds. He sat in a box near the

Giants' dugout and was practically mobbed. He was the town's hero because New York has always had an affinity for Broadway-type characters who are a little sharper than the law.

But now a curious thing happened. The firm of Fallon and McGee, which had expected to do a big business when and if Fallon was acquitted, found itself getting the old go-by. The anticipated rush of clients just failed to materialize. Clients were afraid to ask Fallon to defend them. They were afraid that Hearst would still be gunning for him. That being so, he wouldn't dare pull any tricks. And Fallon without tricks would be like a juggler without Indian clubs.

Fallon, strapped for money, sold the house he and his wife lived in for a fraction of its worth and the couple moved to a small apartment in the Oxford Hotel. He began to hit the bottle so steadily that he was drunk more often than he was sober. He went around town, babbling that David Belasco was going to make a big stage star of him. But by now Belasco, too, was laying off him. Gertrude Vanderbilt gave him money now and then and then went to Europe to fill theatrical engagements.

Some of Fallon's legal enemies—men he had beaten in the courtrooms—sold the Bar Association on the idea that it would be a good move to disbar Fallon. But Fallon, like a phoenix rising from its own ashes, became his old self again—just long enough to argue successfully before the Bar Association that he should not be disbarred.

Once in a while, Fallon would latch on to a case in which he defended a bootlegger. But by now he was so shot with booze that he began to flub the cases and a couple of his bootlegger clients went to Atlanta. He was through but he didn't realize it. The old vanity was still there. He had done it once; he could do it again.

His friend McGraw threw one in his lap—the case of a Giant

player accused of participating in a fixed game. Fallon appeared before Baseball Commissioner Landis to argue the player's case. Landis handed down his decision: the banishment of the player from organized baseball.

One day in the summer of 1926—two years after he had gotten his acquittal in the juror-bribing case—Fallon was holed up in a midtown hotel room. There was a knock on the door. Fallon, thinking it was a bootlegger delivering another quart, opened the door. A jealous woman friend, not a bootlegger, was standing at the door. She too, was carrying liquid in a bottle—acid. She threw it in Fallon's face.

Taken to a hospital, Fallon was found to be seriously burned. Some of the acid had gotten into one eye. It was thought that Fallon would lose the sight of the eye. He had a few dollars in his pocket. He bribed an attendant to go out and bring him in a bottle of whisky. He got high right there in the hospital room.

Fallon got out of the hospital, not only with the sight of the eye saved but with hardly a scar to show for the dose of acid. "It's the luck of the Irish," he told a reporter.

Fallon, who was occasionally stricken by remorse because of the shabby treatment he had given his wife over the years, vowed when he left the hospital that he would never cheat on her again. The woman believed him. They were together, in their apartment in the Oxford, when the New Year of 1927 came in. "*This* year will be different," Fallon said to his wife. "I've been through the worst. And after all, I'm only thirty-nine."

But Fallon's past had more than caught up with him. His shady legal work through the years, his failure to live up to the hopes that his mother had had for him, his failure as a husband, his failure even as a lover—all those elements had combined to drive him to drink. And, once he became an alcoholic, he couldn't pull himself together sufficiently to make up for his past mistakes, even had he sincerely wanted to.

And so, one day in late April of 1927, William Joseph Fallon, the man who just missed genuine greatness, died of a gastric hemorrhage and a heart attack in his rooms in the Oxford Hotel. Hardly any of the fair-weather friends attended the funeral—which was par for the Broadway course. The man who had tossed thousands around like confetti didn't leave even enough to buy a coffin. It didn't come out until later that the handsome coffin that Fallon went away in, dressed in blue serge and wearing a burgundy necktie, was purchased by that rugged Irish friend named John J. McGraw.